Praise for 20 *Things I Know for Sure*

"20 *Things I Know for Sure* is pure food for the soul. Well-earned life experience fills the pages of this book of wisdom. It's a genuine treasure."

—**Caroline Myss**, author of *Anatomy of the Spirit*

"Here is a book that will lift your Spirit and bring you closer to the Self you were meant to be. In these pages, Karen Casey reminds us of the simple truths that can bring us to an ever greater peace of mind."

—**Jon Mundy**, PhD, executive director of All Faith's Seminary, New York City, and author of *A Course in Mysticism and Miracles*

"True to form, Karen Casey's latest book is gentle, honest, instructive, and inspiring. Reading it feels like sitting with her over a cup of tea, absorbing the wisdom drawn from her life experience. I marvel at Karen's ability to convey its truths with her own blend of spiritual understanding and common sense. We would all do well to adopt her "20 Things" as tenets in our own lives—the down-to-earth wisdom and kindness they hold are guaranteed to make every day better."

—**Debra Landwehr Engle**, author of *The Only Little Prayer You Need, Let Your Spirit Guides Speak,* and *Be the Light that You Are*

"Reading the words of Karen Casey is like having a chat with a wise friend. She has lived and practiced everything she writes, so the insights she shares are real and relatable. She walks her talk and that makes her rare and relevant."

—**Beverly Hutchinson McNeff**, founder and president of the Miracle Distribution Center, Anaheim, California

20 Things I Know for Sure

I Know for Sure

Principles for Cultivating a Peaceful Life

KAREN CASEY

Conari Press

This edition first published in 2019 by Conari Press, an imprint of
Red Wheel/Weiser, LLC

With offices at:
65 Parker Street, Suite 7
Newburyport, MA 01950
www.redwheelweiser.com

ISBN: 978-1-57324-744-3

Library of Congress Cataloging-in-Publication Data available upon
request.

Cover design by Kathryn Sky-Peck
Cover image: Tea cup, c.1880, English School, (19th century) /
    The Geffrye Museum of the Home, London, UK / Bridgeman Images
Interior by Deborah Dutton
Typeset in Weiss and Frutiger

Printed in Canada
MAR
10 9 8 7 6 5 4 3 2 1

I want to dedicate this book to my husband, Joe, who has been my constant companion for more than four decades. Our sometimes bumpy road has been made smoother by our willingness to listen and be helpful to one another when either one of us is struggling. I am convinced that we are very intentional partners on this journey.

I also want to dedicate this book to all my fellow travelers in 12-Step rooms. Opening our hearts to one another has made it possible for each one of us to stay on the path to more peaceful lives. I am so grateful for every voice that has reached my ears.

CONTENTS

INTRODUCTION

This book is the culmination of more than forty-three years in Alcoholics Anonymous and Al-Anon, and an equal number of years in search of a connected, peaceful way to live. It represents many years of recommitments to living just this one day, this one moment, just this one breath at a time. And I am still on the search, as a matter of fact.

I frequently wonder whether I would have tried to change the trajectory of my life if I had known where I was heading as a result of the decisions I was making as a young girl—decisions I continued to make long into adulthood. My choices were often extremely risky—some would even say dangerous. Living on the edge appealed to me. A treasured friend "in the rooms" often said: "If we aren't living on the edge, we are taking up too much space." That always made me laugh and it was simply too true for me.

On most days, I believe pretty emphatically that where I have traveled was exactly where I was meant to travel. And yet, I'm seduced by the question: "What if I had not . . . ?"

Then I pass through any number of scenarios I might have sidestepped.

For instance, what if I had not mixed that coke with whiskey at age thirteen? Or given up my virginity at seventeen? What if I had not married my first husband? After all, I had near-daily data from the first date on that he got sloppy drunk every time he got near alcohol. But by then, I also drank too much. I watched him humiliate my family and himself on dozens of occasions. I could have walked away. Perhaps I should have walked away. But a glue held us together. Perhaps the same glue that holds any of us fast to the journey that is calling to us from the day we are born, even when that journey is fraught with pain, uncertainty, and danger. It's a glue we don't understand, but can't get free of.

Carolyn Myss, a spiritual intuitive I had the pleasure of hearing speak many years ago and whom I refer to in the following pages, says in her seminal book *Sacred Contracts* that we have all made agreements—contracts with each and every soul we meet on our journey—prior to "arriving here, in this life." These contracts tie us to a single lesson or set of lessons we agreed to learn and, even more important— *perhaps*—that we agreed to teach one another.

I like this explanation for how we ended up where we find ourselves in any moment that engages our attention. Take, for instance, this very moment, the moment in which you and I have actually crossed paths. We made an agreement. Long ago. I'm quite sure of it. And I'm comforted by it.

Myss' theory has taken the anguish out of all that has happened in my own life. *All of it*—the good and the harrowing. Moreover, it has taken the angst out of what I anticipate may be just around the corner. For there will be more lessons to be learned today, and around every next corner as well.

20 Things I Know for Sure

We can put that thought in the bank and consider it the promise of this life.

In this book, I trace how the power of hindsight, coupled with maturity and recovery from addiction, has changed the way I feel about numerous significant "signposts" along this path that has been mine—signposts that I have come to believe are "the things I know for sure."

Life's meaning has changed for me. Quite significantly. What I experience now is dramatically different from how I experienced life as a child, as a young girl, and as a young adult woman. And the changes in my understanding of so many experiences over the last forty years utterly astound me. But I have distilled from my myriad experiences truths that simply claim me, calm me, and empower me. Truths that point my way forward every day. Truths I have felt compelled to share in numerous books over the last thirty-five years.

The individuals we encounter in life and all the accompanying lessons we learn have not come unbidden. Nary a single person is an accidental visitor on our paths. Discovering how specific experiences and key moments have contributed to what I now embrace as life's ever-evolving meaning thrills me.

Many of these experiences and key ideas will appear and reappear as you move through the chapters in this book. That's quite intentional. Certain ideas impacted my life so profoundly that I believe them worth repeating. In fact, my inner voice wouldn't allow me to mention them only once.

The impact of these ideas and experiences on my own life has also convinced me that my readers can benefit from this repetition. Hearing an idea only once—no matter how good that idea is—never left an indelible mark on me in my lifetime. I can only assume that the same may be true for you. So enjoy hearing my thoughts repeated throughout this book. The repetition will be telling you: *Listen up. This is important. This will make your life more understandable. This idea will ease your journey.*

I am thrilled that you have joined me through these pages. Our meeting is not accidental!

CHAPTER 1

Value Your Relationships

It's only within our relationships that we heal. This seems so obvious, doesn't it? In isolation, we are not faced with encounters of any kind, particularly those we deem unwanted. Living solitary lives seems safe. We feel protected, shielded. No one can hurt us. Many of us choose isolation all too often rather than confront the fear of being with others—any others. Even in instances when we have to cross paths with someone at work or on the street—even with acquaintances—many of us have developed clever ways to shield our vulnerability.

We can recognize this behavior in others as well. At times, it seems endemic. Perhaps social media has contributed to this ever-present condition. But we can't escape the truth that wounds—anyone's wounds—will not heal, cannot heal, unless we allow the "balm" of the presence of others to touch us, to comfort us. The doorway to relationship must be opened. Initially, it may only be propped open, and that's okay. But, as we prop open our own doors, we show others how to prop open theirs as well. Seeing others dare to be open shows us what is possible.

When I review the first four decades of my life, even though I wasn't physically isolated from others, I now see that I never embraced relationships, *of any kind,* as the gift they were. I separated myself even while in the presence of others. I stood aside. I vehemently maintained my position apart—both by choice and by the feeling of exclusion.

Prior to my life as a recovering woman, whenever I was with or simply around someone else, it was always about getting something—generally something that would make me feel valued. Not so invisible. I always made this necessary trade-off in my mind. Always. It didn't even feel like a conscious decision. "Do something for me and just perhaps I'll reciprocate." It was simply the way I navigated through life.

I did this for so many years that it became second nature; it was "me." So I can all too easily recognize the signs when others are navigating through their own lives in much the same way. Scared, hurt people are always looking for signs of acceptance. And just as often, these scared, hurt people don't even recognize the signs because they (we) are so self-absorbed.

Is it strange that so many of us choose to live at arm's length from one another? I think not. Often, our families of origin didn't prepare us for healthy relationships. Using my own family as an example, there was constant tension between my parents that sowed tension throughout our household. We tiptoed around emotions that were always just under the surface, except when my dad's anger erupted. And this became a way of life.

Never seeing honest expressions of love and acceptance at home set the stage for me never knowing how to model that behavior. Actually, I'm embarrassed to say that, far into adulthood, I wasn't particularly conscious of the value of these expressions or of their necessity to the human community or to myself. We don't know what we don't know, and not seeing good role models makes an indelible mark on us.

But we can't continue this practice of always distancing ourselves, of withholding who we have a chance of becoming, if we want to grow, to mature emotionally, to find the joy coupled with love that is inherent in the many thousands of encounters that wear our names. And that's the all-important key: Our encounters with others wear *our* names. This is what being willing to shift how we see and then embrace all relationships—those that are significant as well as those that are fleeting—can offer us. This is where we need to fix our attention. It's within these experiences that we find our true purpose. And that purpose is now, and always has been, to heal and show others that they can heal too.

No Accidents

Any encounter you have wears your name. And your encounters are the next stepping stones of your life. Your opportunities for relationships—of all kinds, everywhere—result directly from the decisions you have previously made, even those decisions you likely do not remember. When you allow this realization to act as the backdrop for all your opportunities—with anyone, anywhere—you remove all fear from your daily plans. Everyone you ever meet "shows up on time." And your intersection is always perfect. Amen.

If only I had known this as a young woman. If you are fortunate, you may perhaps already share this view. And yet I believe, now, that we learn what we need to know at the perfect time in our evolution. And acquiring this information at any time, saves time. We need not be troubled about our journeys—how they meander, how we often stumble because of our confusion—if only we remember: "Ah, yes, this truly is as it should be." We will always get where we need to be. Always. We will always learn what we need to learn. Always. The time it takes isn't what matters. It's our willingness that matters.

This may seem like an oversimplification of our relationships. It's certainly not how I looked at them for the first forty years of my life. In fact, initially, even after realizing this central truth, I couldn't fully embrace it. Too many individuals came rushing into my mind who could not all have been necessary learning partners. Not really. *Could they?* The relative who sexually abused me? The colleague who introduced me to street drugs? The series of strangers who found their way into my bed at the height of my alcoholic madness? Indeed, now I know that they did all have their place in the tapestry I was "instructed" to weave. And I am at peace with each episode, each thread of this tapestry. At peace, at last.

The good news is that the meaning of so many life experiences does change, does become transformed, if and when we are willing to open our minds to new information and new ways of understanding what happened earlier. And this paves the way for our willingness to be transformed again and again, even in the midst of what may be on our horizons right now. Today, I became open. Hallelujah. I hope you are moving in that direction as well.

20 Things I Know for Sure

How I see each relationship now, regardless of how fleeting it may be, is 180 degrees different from how I used to see every one of them. The clerks at the supermarket, the crew mowing the lawn, the UPS delivery man all represent opportunities for me to express attentiveness, acceptance, and kindness. All are necessary experiences in the process of healing each and every relationship.

And the long-standing relationships that I consider significant beyond question allow me to hone the characteristics I was born to embody. Knowing to the depths of my toes that no encounter, even those I have labeled as fleeting, is superfluous to my journey—that no one dances across the screen of my life without a reason—gives me a sense of quiet well-being. Wherever "we" are, regardless of the scenario, is a necessary thread making its contribution to my tapestry. This is a universal truth that can be celebrated by all of us. The tapestry we each are weaving is evidence of our commitment to healing.

Relationships exist for the benefit of both or all parties concerned. "Benefit" is the operative word here. A relationship is not owned by either party, but is rather the link that encourages growth for both people. Actually, it's more far-reaching than that. Every person touched by each party in the relationship can be a beneficiary as well. That idea was beyond my ability to grasp for decades. My insecurities, which were significant, pushed me to cling ever so fearlessly to the partner I'd taken as my hostage, and then attempt to control that person's most minute movements so I'd never be left to fend for myself. I feared abandonment so much that I inadvertently triggered the very thing I feared by my incessant need to put a stranglehold on him, no matter who he was.

I revered relationships for all the wrong reasons. I assumed they were for my sole benefit, my security. From my first serious relationship in high school into the early years of my current marriage, I clung, and clung tightly, lest I be discarded for the next skirt that crossed the room before my partner's eyes. The notion that we had work to do, that our coming together was for a far larger purpose than the one my ego had imagined, was beyond my comprehension. And yet all the "mistakes" I made along the way didn't really throw my journey off course. Detours are normal. Destinations are inviolate. All our lessons are necessary—sometime, someplace.

It has become like a breath of fresh air for me to embrace the idea that my particular lessons will seek me out—if not in one relationship, then in another. Thus the entire meaning of relationships and how they are meant to serve us and humanity has changed significantly for me as I have aged and matured emotionally.

When I began thinking about the underlying topics for this book—the truths that I had come to rely on—I admit that I wasn't sure if they would ring true for others. But being willing to sit and listen has begun to offer me the confidence I needed. I can't promise these truths will satisfy all readers; I can only promise that my own life has been healed as I've grown to embrace them.

This is much like the direction we receive from the God of our understanding on any one day of our lives. Our willingness to listen is what is necessary. Nothing more than that. But nothing less either. I wasn't a listener in my youth.

Nor did I listen very attentively even in the early years of my recovery. My own ego was far too loud, far too busy trying to direct my life and everyone else's as well. It hasn't entirely quit, even now. And it probably never will. But now it takes a back seat far more often than it did earlier in my life.

And I do know that what I am here to learn and do relies on my willingness to listen to the quieter voice in my mind, the one that made the pact with each person on my path. I also know that the primary assignment with each one of these encounters is to listen to that voice, to be attentive and kind and open to whatever information has found its way to me.

That relationships have often been the bane of our existence, as well as necessary teaching tools, should give all of us a moment's pause. We have needed every one of them— those that hurt, regardless of the depth of the wound, right along with those that were joy-filled. When we are in the midst of a relationship experience, we can never decide its value to us now or in the future. All we can know for certain is that it has come because it is necessary. And it will leave its mark, just as every past relationship has done.

My willingness to see each of my relationships—those that are nearly forgotten and those I will never forget, as well as those that continue to captivate me—is the sum and substance of what I need to celebrate about all relationships. It doesn't matter when we come to understand what the real value of a relationship was or is. As a matter of fact, we don't ever have to know a relationship's true value. All we have to accept, finally, is that it was meant for us. For our growth. For our benefit. For our healing. And for the specific contribution we have been born to make.

There are no accidents. There never were any accidental visitors on our paths. And whomever we meet tomorrow is our very next gift. As we are theirs. This I believe whole-heartedly.

CHAPTER 2

Learn from Life

Your past always informs your present, which gives birth to your future. "I'm going to be a working lady. I don't want babies." According to my mom, this was what I insisted when I was about eight. I've been amazed any number of times that my inner self was speaking my truth decades before my adult self caught up. The trajectory of my life actually never did veer in the direction of child-rearing. Like most young girls, I babysat as much as possible. Not reluctantly, but also never because I loved taking care of kids. I did it for the twenty-five cents an hour that I earned. And I still remember how nervous I was when I made the decision to raise my rate to thirty-five cents an hour. Would the parents balk? They did. Recently, I was at a neighborhood gathering and learned that the going rate for babysitting, at least in my neighborhood, is now ten dollars an hour. And no balking!

What I did want as a young girl was independence. I wanted to make my own decisions. I wanted to be in charge. And I wanted distance. In fact, I wanted it from the toddler stage on. According to my older sister, I never shed a tear after tumbling down two flights of stairs onto the cold, hard cement of the basement floor when I was two years old. When she came running to pick me up to comfort me, I pushed her away. I didn't want help. Had I already determined that putting my trust in others wasn't wise? Sometimes it still troubles me. Why did I push love away when it was so freely offered?

Not unlike millions of young people, then and now, I knew I wanted to be different in many ways from my family, and specifically from my sisters initially. It wasn't that I didn't like them; on the contrary, I did. I simply wanted a "bigger" life. I didn't want to work at the tiny corner grocery across the street from our house that was owned by our uncle.

It was assumed I would follow in their footsteps, but I adamantly refused. I wanted to work downtown, in a department store, where I could chart my own path unsupervised by any family member. So at age fifteen, to the chagrin of my parents, I marched into the largest department store in Lafayette, lied on the application, claiming to be sixteen, and got my first real job. I was a salesgirl! With a time card and an employee discount. I had arrived!

Even though I had a job I loved and was good at, I lacked confidence in so many other areas of my life. Was I genuinely liked? Was my boyfriend planning to reject me? Was I making the grade with my friends and in my classes? Was I going to be truly special to one man someday?

Truthfully, that was the all-important concern. Would someone want to marry me? I hate to admit how focused I was on that, but it undergirded my decision to go to college. That's where marriages were made in the Fifties. I had seen it happen with my sisters. In that one regard, I did want to be like them. I did want to be chosen, and who "the chooser" was wasn't even important. I didn't want to be left standing on the sidelines as the bridesmaid again and again.

My early years foreshadowed who I was to become—something that is true for all of us, I believe. As is true of most young girls, I played teacher to my dolls and then to my friends. And I eventually became one: first an elementary school teacher and then an instructor on a college campus. My evolution was perfect. I was always in the right place at the right time.

Right Place, Right Time

You will always be where you need to be for the next right thing to happen. This is a truth you can count on. It's the unquestionable certainty for everyone, everywhere, actually. And you need not even know this for it to be true.

My first book was a testament to that as well. In grammar school, I began writing stories about a girl with a life more interesting than mine. Most important, her parents didn't argue all the time. There wasn't an undercurrent of tension in her home that touched each person. Living "through" this fictional family gave me palpable relief. This family also gave me direction and hope, and a determination to reach beyond where I was.

Every book I have written over the last three and a half decades has grown out of my determination to cre-ate a new reality—the very same determination I had as a nine-year-old. I realize now that these stories were akin to the vision boards I would be inspired to create as a young recovering woman. Vision boards are like the story boards that screenwriters use to create dramatic plots. The difference is that vision boards can help to project a real, not a fictional, narrative. With vision boarding, I believed that *if I could see it, I could make it real*. If I could write it, it could materialize in my life and help others too.

The most profound experience I had with vision boarding, and why I believe in its power, happened the very first time I tried it. Every picture I placed on my first carefully considered board did, in fact, manifest. One picture showed a woman playing tennis; another showed her playing golf; a third picture showed her wearing a business suit and carrying a briefcase. And central to them all was a woman standing next to a dark-haired man. He was building bookcases against a wall in a home. A little more than a year later, I realized that the dark-haired man was the man who was to become my husband. And he actually built the wall of bookcases for me. As I watched him do it, I fully understood the power of envisioning an experience I wanted as my own.

A vision board's power can be remarkable. I had never really taken to heart what I had heard so many others say about sending out to the universe that which we hope to experience. Do we actually need vision boards to send out our requests? Probably not, but the process of making one creates its own magnetism. It requires being pensive, prayerful, actively hopeful, and expectant. All four of these qualities lend weight to the request we are making. And the creation of the board is our invitation to the universe to manifest our vision, along with our decision to let the fretting go.

While preparing for my final oral exam for my doctorate, I didn't opt to make a vision board. I had recently read a fascinating article in *Psychology Today* about the power of meditative envisioning. As a result, I instead sat for thirty minutes in quiet meditation every day for a month, "seeing myself" in the room where I knew the exam would take place, answering each question asked by my six committee members. We smiled and nodded as we talked. On the day of the exam, I walked into that room feeling quite comfortable. *I had been there before. I was ready to proceed.* And I passed the exam, earning my degree.

I find it rather curious, in hindsight, that my stories as a youngster could be considered juvenile attempts to send ideas out to the universe. Those stories didn't actually materialize as written. After all, I was quite busy fulfilling the many pacts I had made with many carefully selected learning partners in real life. But the process of creating those make-believe families had an impact, nonetheless. It trained me to listen to the voice within, to trust its words, to let them comfort me.

Nothing that we ever do is wasted. Everything that calls to us—whether it be an idea or an experience or a person—does so for a reason that will become known to us at the right time. For me, the call to write was born when I was nine years old, and that call never died.

I was brash as a young girl. And fearful too. I came by both of these characteristics honestly, a saying so often heard from the lips of my dad. I feared abandonment from the moment I took notice of others on my path. Would they be long-time or fleeting friends? Would they choose someone else over me? This very thing happened, as a matter of fact, when I was in the sixth grade. A classmate and I had been best friends for three years. Every day after school, I pedaled as fast as I could to her house to hang out. And then another girl moved into our neighborhood and became a classmate.

Instantly, I was afraid that she would come between my best friend and me. My worst fears materialized. No matter how fast I pedaled to my friend's house, she and our new classmate had already gone for a ride. The devastation I felt then was repeated many times throughout my life, particularly in my relationships with men. As I mentioned earlier, I tried to hold on to people, but my clinging drove them away. It happened more than once, but the most devastating time was when my first husband left me.

Fortunately, when I got into recovery, I went to a counselor and the first words out of her mouth were: "You were abandoned in the womb." I was both shocked and confused. How could she know that and what did it mean? Truthfully, I was immediately suspect. There were crystals hanging from the ceiling and pillows instead of couches all over the room. Fortunately, I was young enough then to get up and down from the floor—something I can no longer easily accomplish.

The counselor was insistent that I had been abandoned in the womb, a common syndrome with recovering women, she said. I certainly did identify with the abandonment diagnosis, but not the womb. And then, about a year later, my mom and I had a talk that changed my life completely—and hers as well.

"Tell me about your life, Mother." I was fulfilling an assignment for a family of origin class, not expecting much of a response. She seldom provided much detail about her life, and in particular about her past. Her general response was always: "I can't remember." Instead, a flood of tears began to flow. "I never felt like a good wife or a good mother, and I didn't want you when I was pregnant with you." Bingo! I had been abandoned in the womb. In those few words, the seed of my discontent, which gave rise to my need to cling to others, emerged. My fear, indeed, had roots—deep roots. The information gave me hope that I'd finally be able to let go.

But the additional gift from that exchange with my mother was her freedom from a secret she had carried for more than thirty-seven years. She could never have told my dad how she felt. In the era in which she grew up, she could never have told any one, in fact. Her shame and guilt had festered for decades. That she was able to tell me released her and opened the door to a bond that comforted both of us for the rest of our years together. We cried long and hard together and, from that moment on, I was so grateful she was my mom.

Speaking truth about the past as well as the present unleashes a power for good, for spiritual growth, for universal connection that moves each one of us—all 7.5 billion of us—into a rhythm that comforts all of humanity. Does this seem like an extravagant claim? Think again. What affects one of us does, indeed, affect all of us. My mother's words changed me; they changed her. And my spiritual journey has convinced me that they left no soul untouched. Not one.

I continued to learn things about my family when I spoke with my dad about his life. I posed the very same question. His response stunned me: "I have been afraid every day of my life." To the rest of us, his success and dominance in our family didn't look like fear. In fact, his eruptions over the smallest incidents looked more like bullying than fear. In the intervening years, I have come to understand the connection between the two, however. But his feelings of fear had their roots in his childhood, as is true for most of us.

My father's explanation for his fear wasn't complicated, but it saddened me, particularly when I realized how it had infected how he looked at himself and everyone of us too. As a six-year-old, he was mowing his family's lawn and accidentally cut off the tips of two of his younger brother's fingers. His parents weren't home, but they came running when they heard and he was severely punished. From that moment forward, being perfect was the requirement imposed on him by his parents. And then he demanded it of himself and of all of us as well. If my mother overcooked the eggs, she was shamed. If my younger brother couldn't catch a ball pitched to him by my dad, he was ridiculed. When he couldn't read without stumbling, which was a constant occurrence, he was a "dumb bunny." And on and on it went.

I fought back to no avail. I felt as if one of us in the family had to defend my mother and younger brother. For years, we battled, my father and I. Even after I left home, our battling continued. Hearing his story did soften my heart, however. His demons held sway over his life forever. Unlike the relief my mom seemed to get from her revelation, I didn't sense that my father felt any freedom from actually admitting his "secret." I'm not sure he even realized how freed he could have been. Anger had been his companion for too long to let it go on its merry way. But his story freed me. And it allowed me to forgive him and myself for my years of judging him. Expecting perfection from yourself and others is a heavy burden. He was weighed down by it for all eighty-six years of his life.

That we can glean greater meaning about our own lives, in particular how we perceive them as they unfold, is one of the many blessings of being attentive to those individuals who have "been called" to join us on our journeys. My story needed my mom and dad. And theirs needed me as well. That's the beauty of our unfolding lives. The pain and confusion we experience are part of the learning curve, even in those moments that feel intolerable. I'm grateful that I understand and can accept that my brother's pain at the hands of my dad was part of his chosen journey too.

As I've said already, nothing on our journeys is superfluous—past, present, or future. Every experience fits snugly into its perfect place like a piece in a jigsaw puzzle. As we near the end of our journeys, as is the case for me, it's far easier to breathe easily and say: "Now I see." What a comfort it is, in fact, to understand—finally—how every experience in my life was so very necessary to transport me here, to you, to this point in time.

CHAPTER 3

Just Open the Door

Wherever we are is where we are meant to be. This was certainly true for me as I walked into my first Al-Anon meeting in 1974. I could not have guessed how the direction of my life was about to change on that night. A group of two dozen unsuspecting men and women were about to share with me a simple plan that was going to change my perspective forever. It didn't happen immediately, of course, but something quite unexpected did happen that first night. I felt a calmness I had never before known. And I felt a whisper of hope. I walked out of that meeting with the feeling that my life could actually change. And for the better.

The folks in the group also made a point of saying that it wasn't possible for me to change others. They had tried. I wasn't convinced, however. I was sure that I could pull off what none of them had succeeded in doing. How arrogant and shortsighted I was. But also quite normal for a newcomer to a program like Al-Anon.

So for the next fews years, even though I was devoted to Al-Anon and, by 1976, to AA as well, my attempts to change others so that I would feel content and secure ran my life. I focused on holding people hostage and trying to control their every move. Nothing I heard at my Al-Anon and AA meetings actually broke through my wall of resistance. Indeed, I was a very slow learner.

The slogan "Let Go and Let God" hung on the wall of nearly every 12-Step room I entered. But it simply didn't register with me. It sounded nice, but its profound meaning went right over my head. I didn't get that it was a suggestion for a practice I could adopt. That it was one of the ways to a peaceful life utterly escaped me.

My journey with God wasn't an easy one. Every meeting I went to felt so comforting. I loved them. I went to lots of them every week. Following each meeting, a group of us found a place for coffee or supper and I felt secure, trusting that I was safe in the hands of a loving God. And loving friends.

Then I went home. I never felt God's presence at home. I often felt frantic, in fact, wondering how others so easily connected with the Higher Power we all spoke about in meetings. Why did I feel so alone as soon as I was by myself? I really didn't talk about my dilemma at meetings or to friends. I guess I didn't want others to know what a failure I felt I was. Having others look at me as someone who "got it" seemed important. In reality, I didn't get it. Not at all. I was scared most of the time. And I understood exactly nothing. But I didn't let on.

Not much changed for me in early recovery, actually. I clung to folks and to meetings. But I was still terrified when surrounded by my own four walls. And yet, I functioned quite well in some arenas. I taught my classes at the university; I went to my graduate courses and excelled. And I went to lots of meetings. They were my safe haven. Until they weren't. After about eighteen months in recovery, I was finally bent on finding relief. The idea of drinking didn't call to me. Dying did. And I made a plan.

Thoughts of suicide haunted me throughout my life. Even as a child, I dreamed about the relief that might come if I simply disappeared. I was never frightened by these thoughts. When I took the Minnesota Multiphasic Personality Inventory while in school, the psychiatrist reported that I was suicidal. To which I casually responded: "Well, everyone is." She quickly corrected me, saying that mentally healthy people are not suicidal. I didn't believe her.

A day came when I was more overwhelmed with fear than usual, and I knew there was an easy way out. I felt ready. And a calmness settled over me. I gathered my bath towels and sat at the kitchen table in my small one-bedroom apartment. I rolled the towels carefully, just so. I wanted them to prevent gas from escaping under the closed windows. It was a very old building and none of the windows were airtight. When I finished rolling the last towel, I heard a gentle knock at my door. I ignored it. But then the knock came again, less gentle this time. I quietly walked over to the door and asked: "Who's there?"

An unfamiliar voice answered: "Pat. We have an appointment to discuss your finances." I was mystified. Not only did I not remember anyone named Pat, but I lived paycheck to paycheck. I was certain she had made a mistake and said so. But she was insistent, calling me by name. So I opened the door. Rather brashly, she came in and pulled out her daily planner. Sure enough, my name was there, where she pointed. Uninvited, she walked into my kitchen. It was only then that she paused and seemed to take notice of my demeanor. "Is there something wrong?" she asked.

I explained that I was very depressed. That I was an alcoholic and felt as if I were alone in the universe. She nodded. She seemed to understand. I continued to talk and she silently listened. And then she shared with me how she had suffered from depression as well, as had her alcoholic husband. She described how she had sought explanations along with solutions. For the next thirty minutes, she talked and I quietly listened. I was both mesmerized and amazed.

"What you are experiencing has a name. It's called 'chemicalization,'" she said. "The ego is trying to hold you hostage on the dark side of the deep abyss you are hanging over. But God is waiting on the other side for you. He sees you. He wants you to trust Him. It's your choice to let go of the old fears and reach across, taking the outstretched hand of God, who has always been there. It's all explained in a book by Catherine Ponder," she said. "The title is *The Dynamic Laws of Healing*."

I was stunned by how her soothing words so quickly comforted me. Then she stood, turned to me, and said: "You are going to be fine. Trust me. Trust God." And she turned toward the door. Not one word about finances had been uttered. But I knew her job was complete. Before she got to the door, she turned back once more and, with outstretched arms, gave me a warm hug. "You will be fine." And out the door she went.

I never saw Pat again. I didn't doubt who she really was, however. She had been sent. And I had opened the door. I have never forgotten the power of having a guardian angel come calling. Not only that, but my experience has convinced me that we are always surrounded by these angels guiding us on our paths, directing traffic, at the perfect time. We need not know this or even fully believe it for it to be true, but I do think we have all sensed their presence at one time or another.

Angels Everywhere

Angels give guidance when you are willing to receive it. Can you remember a time when perhaps you drew back from a dangerous experience or stepped back onto the curb as a bus approached? These experiences occur when you open the door to the guidance you need and deserve.

The fellowships of Alcoholics Anonymous, Al-Anon, and other 12-Step programs, coupled with numerous spiritual pathways, have turned millions of lives around. Truly, no one has to keep suffering if he or she wants a different life. But each one of us has to be willing to change—be willing to want to change. We have to be willing to open the door—to listen to the voice of the One who has come to help us change, in the right way, at the right time, and in the right place.

I had no idea I was headed for a change of any kind when I wandered into first one and then another 12-Step program. I delusionally thought my life was going pretty well. In fact, it was remarkably exciting on occasion. I easily lived in denial of how emotionally unmanageable my life had become. I loved the classes I was teaching at the university. I, most surprisingly, was a straight-A doctoral student.

And I loved the wild crowd I ran with. Bars were "my thing." Jack Daniels and drugs were "my thing." Living on the edge was "my thing." I was not looking to change anything. Not one thing. But change came to me anyway.

The importance of being open to the changes that we were "born to make" is one of the great bits of wisdom I have come to cherish as I have aged. We rarely know where we are headed until we have already turned a corner. And isn't that a beautiful awareness. The intricate way that life unfolds for each of us has been perfectly orchestrated. We will "play whatever tune is ours," in unison with other "members of the band." I love that image. I love its truth even more.

I'm constantly amazed that so many of us live for so many years in total darkness about how and why our lives unfold so perfectly. Great sources of wisdom have told us for eons that nothing happens in this world accidentally—nothing. But most of us doubt it. Or fail to even consider it at all. But when we believe this central truth, wholly and unabashedly, we can diminish the fear regarding any uncertainty over what may be coming.

Years of clinging to this belief have now convinced me of its truth. That conviction didn't come easily, but hindsight helped. So did the realization that one quite perfect experience after another has invited me in as a participant. Am I implying that each experience was easy? On the contrary. But as I have entered my eighth decade, I can see the pattern my life had to take in order for me to be called to sit here with all of you today.

Not one experience—whether one that I barely survived or one that I celebrated wholeheartedly—was superfluous to the finished product that is my life. And there will be many more experiences to come, in fact, each one as perfect as every one from the past has been. The tumble down the basement steps when I was two, the family sexual predator who invaded my space when I was ten, my experience of walking across the stage to receive my doctoral degree were all pieces that fit perfectly into my personal jigsaw puzzle.

In each experience, I had a protector. I believe that adamantly. But our protectors don't prevent us from discovering our lessons, some of which are quite painful. Instead, they help us to recognize them so that we can move on to the next chapter of our lives. They lead us. And we follow. They encourage us to open the door. We may not have known the truth of this, but that doesn't negate it. Guidance is present. Always.

Nor is any one of us without "an assignment"—a connection to everyone who crosses our paths. Just as Pat was on assignment to me, we each have our own assignments as well. Millions of them over a lifetime. And what an awesome responsibility and *opportunity* this gives us.

The good news is that these assignments, these connections, give purpose to our lives, moment by moment. Early on in my spiritual journey, I was consumed by the question: What is God's will for me? Prior to recovery, I had never considered the question, but I was sure it had to be something big—like undertaking a new job, or moving to another city or country, or walking away from certain relationships and into others. Any one of those things might have eventually fit into my "bigger tapestry." But God's will, in the moment, was far simpler. It was to show up lovingly on another person's path and be kind, to show the way. No real thought has to go into the action. Just willingness. Simple willingness.

Believing that this is my job description has brought simplicity to my life in those moments when I get highjacked by my ego and begin to struggle over the next "right thing" to do or say or think. The ego speaks extremely loudly and has no intention, ever, of letting us be peaceful. It thrives on chaos and control. It wants us to be angry and frustrated. It demands fear and resistance from us.

The ego is the antithesis of the peace we find when we *let go and let God*. It creates the insanity that drives people into conflict, neighborhoods into turmoil, countries into combat. However, there is a simple solution that can change the direction of each person—a solution that can shift the universe, in fact. Simply open the door to the possibility of peace in your life. Be someone who fulfills God's will. Be the presence of love wherever you go in this next moment. You will be in the perfect place at the perfect time to do it, and the people you find there will be present specifically to receive your love. Remember, wherever you are is where you are meant to be.

CHAPTER 4

Surrender to Spirit

Spirit guides; ego controls. Spirit is real. It's eternal, of course, and I believe it's our sole and essential essence. Unlike ego, which pushes to control us every moment, Spirit seeks to guide us. In the 1975 book, *A Course in Miracles*, Helen Schucman, the scribe who intently listened to the voice of Jesus for seven years, presents a program for spiritual transformation that has complemented my thinking for nearly three decades. Jesus shared with Helen that the greatest miracle we can achieve in our lives is to gain a full awareness of love's presence. According to the principles of the Course, Spirit is absolutely *all* that is real about us. And the realization that Spirit is unending is an awareness that constantly blesses me.

I find this principle both comforting and, at long last, quite believable. What our eyes feast on are illusions, often amazingly "real" illusions. People or trees; dogs or horses; cars or houses; mountains or lakes; our bodies as well as our neighbors' bodies. These are all illusions that we have projected into this classroom of life that the ego has conjured up around us.

What a startling and elusive idea this was for me when I first encountered it a few decades ago! How could the ego have that much power? But the ego, according to the Course, always speaks first; it's always loudest; and it's always wrong. And we all too willingly let it hold us hostage, drawing us away from the quieter, kinder path of Spirit. But if the only thing that's actually real is Spirit, how can the ego so easily commandeer our attention? That's its power. That's the power of the illusion it has created.

Spirit never leaves; it's within us always. But it's not pushy. It's not insistent. It's available when we are willing to remember its presence. And it is eternal. But we must do our part; we must be willing to turn in its direction and to open the door. Again and again.

Our bodies, which appear to be real—we can touch them as they carry us from place to place, after all—serve us in only one way. They transport us from one specifically chosen encounter to another in this elaborate classroom of illusions. That's their soul purpose. This is certainly not an unworthy purpose, because all our encounters are specific to the greater purpose we each have that mirrors what we agreed to experience before waking up in this classroom. However, it's imperative that we remember that nothing about these illusions is actually real—except to the ego. Nothing about them will last except in our fearful minds, which are also the ego's creation. And yet they serve a purpose, one that's necessary to the Whole of us.

Classroom of Illusions

Every experience you have in the classroom of the ego is contracted for—agreed to. Your "learning partners" are specifically selected and are as necessary to your journey as you are to theirs. Each encounter experienced—those that feel significant as well as those that seem merely fleeting—are individual threads in the tapestry you were born to weave. Remember: There are no accidental encounters. You are always where you are meant to be, meeting those you are supposed to meet.

Spirit is the primary fact of our existence. And here is the truly mind-bending truth about it: Spirit remains at "home." In fact, it never actually leaves its home, which is heaven. *And we are still there, at home, as well!* Regardless of how the ego makes it seem—and it works very hard to convince us otherwise— *we are still there.* Accepting this as an indisputable truth gives me great peace now, although it also gave me many moments of disbelief when I first encountered it. How can I, how can we, be in two places at once? "At home" with Spirit and in this classroom of the ego. How indeed?

Of course, the simple answer is that we can't be in both places at once. And yet this classroom looks and feels so real. My body looks and feels so real. And yours does too. I, for one, appreciate the constant reassurance of others who share the same spiritual principles that guide my life—that we are Spirit. Period. Still "at home." Period.

We "wear bodies" in this classroom simply so that we can gather the knowledge we seem to have forgotten. Yet, in reality, nothing we ever knew as Spirit is gone; it is only temporarily hidden from us by the ego, which glories in the chaotic conundrum in which we find ourselves, here and now. The ego has taken us hostage and we have unknowingly succumbed.

This particular principle had to be one of "the twenty things I know for sure" because of the comfort it offers me every time it comes to mind. As a matter of fact, that was the test for each of the twenty principles that comprise this book. How much peace do I feel each time I quietly consider each one of these principles? Peace was and is the inherent gift that lies within each principle given here. And peace is the gift I hunger for in my own classroom of the ego.

Believing that Spirit is real and eternal also allows me to continue communicating in my own quiet way with each of my loved ones who have "gone home," and that feels extremely necessary to me. Because they and we are all Spirit, no channel is needed to connect us. We simply *are* in direct communication through our unending Oneness. These loved ones are the "hovering angels" who grace my life—and yours as well, if you choose to share this belief.

Like so much else about Spirit, Oneness was initially a hard concept for me to grasp. We look so separate. We feel so separate. And in the classroom of the ego, every occurrence supports the concept of separateness. My own seduction by the ego and the transference of its idea that we are separate individuals in constant competition with one another was quite complete. I was held hostage by the ego and its ugly misinformation for the first half of my life. And I didn't even know it!

And yet that isn't the truth about us. We are One. We are eternal. And Spirit is the whole of us, regardless of what the ego tries to project.

What a glorious truth this is.

Remember: The ego always speaks first. And it's the loudest. And it's always wrong. This makes it an extremely subtle foe. All we have to do is look around us or turn on the news to see the evidence of its work. We hear of young people who are gunned down in a small town. There are battlegrounds everywhere. But if we remember the truth about ourselves—that we are Spirit, not ego, and that we are One—we can eventually turn the tide and transform the ego's classroom from a nightmare into a "happy dream."

This may seem beyond the capacity of humankind, but Spirit is all-powerful. And Spirit stands at the ready to support us when we open the door to it—now, this moment, and forever.

CHAPTER 5

Turn Your Back on Fear

Every struggle in your life can be relinquished. This statement seemed incomprehensible to me when I first heard it. I had been struggling with people since I was a child. It began with my dad. I simply wasn't going to be told what to do when it ran counter to my wishes. Truth be told, I was spring-loaded to fight back, even when he was right—which was not all that uncommon.

For years, my reaction to my dad seemed unalterable. He was often angry, something that set me on edge because, when he was angry, all of us became targets for his ugly criticism. As a child, I criticized right back. As a young girl, I argued and felt protective of my mom and younger brother, who were my father's primary targets. Eventually, my penchant for arguing turned to almost daily angry outbursts that were not unlike his own.

My two older sisters seemed to escape the family struggle that I experienced—a realization I only came to as a grown woman. But my mom and my brother and I were engaged in a drama that played out almost every evening.

It was many years later that I learned of the fear that lay beneath my dad's anger. And I have come to believe that fear always lies at the root of our anger. It's created by the ego, which loves to be in charge of every aspect of our lives. Both my dad and I were held hostage by our egos. It wasn't a pretty sight. Our dance wasn't a smooth one. And as I grew older, I repeated this dance in relationship after relationship.

When my dad told me, through clenched teeth, about the childhood experience that had initiated his life-long fear, it saddened me and dramatically changed how I looked at him. His parents' rage had colored every day of his life and, when I tried to comfort him, he couldn't hear me. He wouldn't hear me.

Later, my dad and I talked about his work. He had been a banker, a successful one. I had felt so proud to tell my friends where he worked when I was young. I was more than a little sad when he said he went to that job full of fear every day, afraid that he would make a mistake that would cast a long shadow over his professional reputation. Nothing I could say or do could shake his resolve that his own perfection was a must. I finally understood why he was always so tough on all of us. We were ordinary humans who made mistakes, a fact in which he could find no peace.

Because fear is at the heart of so many disagreements—I'm inclined to say all of them, actually—it isn't easy for us to relinquish our position in an argument. Fear takes a hold of us and won't let go. The ego fights us at every turn to keep us in the grip of fear. It loves cultivating that fear because that keeps it in control. But simply coming to believe, however slowly, that we can survive the decision to let go of our struggles, regardless of what initiated them, is like a gift we didn't know was coming. The prospect of letting go of our struggles is so unexpected that we doubt it can be possible at first—and sometimes that doubt lingers for years.

When I first heard the phrase "Let Go and Let God," I shook my head in mild disgust. I was sitting in an Al-Anon meeting. The year was 1974. I didn't believe in God at that time, nor did I think there was anything to be gained by letting go of any situation in which I was enmeshed. I was intent on controlling outcomes and people! My lack of success didn't keep me from trying, nor believing, that if I could only come up with the correct rationale, I'd eventually change others.

I was in the right place that night, but it actually took many years before the meaning of "letting go" got through to me. Practice, continuous daily practice, is what finally changes our minds, then our behavior. I had many years of spoiled relationships to practice on before I began to really get the gist of letting go. And then, it took more practice still. Needless to say, I'm still practicing.

Being able to embrace the concept of relinquishing any situation that is causing inner turmoil, or letting go of a person who isn't behaving the way we want them to, offers the greatest sense of freedom we can ever experience in this classroom of life. To think we can do it once and for all the first time we try, however, is unrealistic. My experience has shown me that old habits and old fears die hard. The focus many of us have on other people and how our lives would be better if only they would change can be extremely seductive.

And yet, change we can. Letting go of people and situations has finally become easier for me. Some days, I still falter—but that's okay. My resolve is constant. And that's all that matters. The time it takes us to achieve this freedom isn't really relevant. We know without a doubt that, to get good at anything—anything at all—we must be willing to do the hard work. The good news is that our willingness to do that work is met more than halfway by Spirit, which dwells in us always.

Practice, Practice, Practice

The idea that you never travel alone, but are always One with Spirit, is not an easy concept to embrace. Your ability to let go of struggles and reject fear comes from the commitment you make to practice—just like learning how to play golf or the clarinet or the piano. It is only through constant attention to this commitment that you can finally turn your back on the fears through which the ego controls you.

In my case, I had discarded any notion of a God long ago, so the suggestion that all aspects of life would be easier if I chose to acknowledge His Presence wasn't very appealing. But so much about my life was painful, not at all peaceful, and ultimately pretty self-destructive. Giving in to the idea of a Presence who was willing to help finally seemed to make sense.

Had I done it sooner, I would have been relieved of lots of pain. However, what I believe now is that I "came to believe" at the right time. In fact, I have come to believe that everything that happens in your life and mine happens only when the time is right.

Does it make sense to revisit all the old relationships that I strangled because of my inability to let go? Or to re-experience the struggles I so often initiated or the fears that held me hostage? I think not. I've concluded that letting the past be past—it's said that even God can't change the past—is the key to a life of contentment. Being free to live this moment with the knowledge that we can walk together in Spirit, unfettered by the desire to make those we meet be other than who they are, assures that we can all walk the path of peace.

Now in my eighth decade, I have embraced at last the true value, the unending value, of letting others be. I have learned to turn my back on my fears and let all situations I encounter be as well. I know this means that my remaining years will be as peaceful as I am willing for them to be. Was time wasted? For sure. Does that matter? Not in the least. Now is the perfect time for me to rejoice that this principle has called my name.

CHAPTER 6

Open Your Heart to Love

A Course in Miracles teaches that every loving thought is true, and that everything else is an appeal for healing and help, regardless of its form. I've been grateful every day since beginning my study of the Course more than three decades ago that it gave me such a simple tool for quickly assessing every situation that involves me and all my "learning partners" on this journey we have chosen to share. Indeed, I have come to think of this particular principle as a guide for interpreting absolutely every personal encounter I have on a daily basis.

If what I experience with a friend or even with a complete stranger isn't loving, I know immediately that they are in need of some form of healing and that their words or actions are an appeal for help. And there is only one kind of help to offer in any adversarial situation—an expression of love, in some form. There are myriad expressions of love we can choose from. Sometimes even a gentle nod or a silent prayer can serve to give succor and support.

This principle has proved invaluable to me over the years. It assures me that I will never be at a loss about how to respond in any setting, as long as I abide by it. Of course, that's the key. I have to make the choice to let this principle guide my thoughts, my words, and, even more important, my actions. And making this choice isn't always what I want to do. Impulsively reacting to what seems like someone else's attack, real or imaginary, is far more appealing at times.

Remember: The ego always speaks first and loudest, and it's always wrong. And it always pushes us to create chaos where none need be. Far too often, we allow the ego to take charge of our actions. And no one is the better for it. No one. Ever.

For example, we have all been cut off in traffic or treated in a curt way by a clerk or another shopper at the grocery store, or even by a friend who may be troubled about some situation. Maybe a family member has blamed you for something that you clearly had nothing to do with. You can respond in kind to this behavior—and have often done so, no doubt—heightening an already tense situation. Or you can step back and consider the possibility that your relative or acquaintance is simply having a difficult day and needs a more loving response from you—the kind of response that can turn that person's day around and keep yours on an even keel as well.

Being able, and willing, to help someone in trouble is truly the "assignment" each one of us is here to complete. Mother Teresa once said: "Be kind to everyone and start with the person standing next to you." What a simple solution for every circumstance that ails us, worldwide.

No one we encounter has mistakenly ended up on our path. *No one*. As Myss tells us, we agreed to whatever experience we shared, and its accompanying lesson, before we "arrived here." And we will learn from our experience if we *lean into it*. But it's likewise true that we can decline these lessons at any given moment if we feel unready to learn them. These lessons will be repeated, perhaps at a later time with the same partner or with an entirely new one. The single thing we can count on is that *the opportunity for learning will return*.

In fact, the person challenged to learn is ultimately not as important as the lesson itself. Our journey is divine. We need not fret. What we need to experience is ours *and it will find us*. This is a gift, not a threat—one that will usher us into the next right awareness.

I never took the many opportunities I had to stop trying to control my first husband and numerous partners who came after him. But in my current marriage, I have surrendered to "that call." The result has been a far more peaceful existence, for my husband and for me. Do I surrender my need to control in every instance? Sadly, no. But letting go even once a day contributes to a far better life. Actually, to a far better universe as well.

Accepting the necessity of all the encounters that we experience and the lessons they offer certainly has the capacity to make my life and yours more peaceful—and hopefully the lives of all our fellow travelers as well. We really do have the choice to say, "Ah, yes. I understand. And I am willing to accept what calls to me." And then move forward.

When I was first introduced to the idea from *A Course in Miracles* that every loving thought is true and everything else is an appeal for healing and help, I was in a Course study group and I wanted to argue the point with the facilitator. I found the words to be so cut and dried. The statement was just too simplistic. I was looking for more complicated explanations for my frequent discomfort in situations involving others. After all, I was nearing completion of a doctorate! Surely there was more to understanding our encounters than this explanation offered. Little did I know that I was subtly being prepared for a major ego adjustment. And I didn't recognize it at all. Not for some time, actually.

As I grow older—and hopefully wiser in some ways—this truth now offers me palpable relief and joy. For most of my life, I fretted over everything that everyone around me was doing, or not doing. I was the hovering, unwanted "police," butting into business that was seldom my own—with family, friends, and, heaven forbid, even strangers. And although I pretended otherwise, none of my interference in the lives of others was evidence of love, but rather of my own need to control—my need for personal security, actually, that could also be interpreted as a need for spiritual healing.

These days, I fondly treasure what a good friend from Al-Anon said in a meeting a number of years ago: "There are two kinds of business; my business and none of my business." I had never before drawn a distinction between the two. What a wake-up call these words were. And they still guide me on a daily basis.

Do I back off from situations that are not my business? Unfortunately, not always—even though this friend's words may be ringing in my ears. And what I have learned is that, when I don't back off, it's because I feel my security is threatened. My interference, my attempt to control, derives simply from the fact that I am afraid. Like my dad. My need for healing in that moment supersedes my willingness to trust that God is in charge. No one is exempt from that need on

20 Things I Know for Sure

occasion. Fear overwhelms each of us at times. And we need not feel ashamed.

Perhaps you are still wondering what "every loving thought is true" actually means and if it can be helpful to you. I was stymied initially as well. And then I learned from others I trusted that "God" could be equated with love and everything that emanates from Him can be accepted as true. Thus, every loving thought expressed by someone on your path is true because it is a God-inspired expression. Deciding what you will do with all the unloving thoughts you encounter is where your real work begins.

Stick to the Plan

Any unloving thought or word or action is simply one of the opportunities you were born to address. In each instance, you are merely carrying out your own part in a plan you agreed to. This principle can provide a great roadmap for your journey through this life. *You are where you need to be, meeting whomever you need to meet, to experience love or the call for love in each instance.* Period. Life actually is simpler than we make it. Isn't it?

Putting into practice all that I have outlined here is your daily assignment. It may sound daunting. Yet opening your heart to each person on your path is all you really need to do. And when we do that, we recognize the loving thoughts nestled in among the cries for healing and help. We need never be at a loss for the kind of response that's called for. Never. And when we remember that each cry is an opportunity we agreed to embrace, we can sit back confidently and trust in the process of our lives.

All the personal "truths" I share in this book, are, of course, drawn from my own experiences wandering, sometimes stumbling, through life. And it may require some willingness on your part to consider any of them helpful. That's okay. It's been my goal as a writer, beginning with *Each Day a New Beginning* in 1982, to share as clearly as possible my own experiences, my strengths, and my hopes so my readers can see my own process for living life. As I have aged, my process has grown simpler, finally distilling down to the twenty principles I share with you here to help you live with an open heart.

Choosing the simpler path probably makes sense to everyone my age. I continue to be astounded by the fact that I have lived to be eighty. How could my life have slipped so quickly through my fingers? But my awareness of the passage of time has certainly prompted me to want to be more attentive to it, and thus to all the people who are quite intentionally traveling with me, offering an expression of love or seeking some form of healing.

My hope in this chapter has been to make you comfortable with all these ideas that I have grown to trust so completely. My goal has been to act as a guide. And that's your purpose as well. Regardless of your age or station in life, you are here to help. And accepting that role takes the guesswork out of the many options that may stand before you on any given day as you awake.

Be helpful. Those two words say it all, don't they? When you respond in a loving manner to every soul who crosses your path, you fulfill God's will completely. From my perspective, there is no better way to "show the way" than to be helpful and express the love for which we all yearn.

Finally, there is no better way to live a peaceful life than deciding to be helpful. In the tiniest of ways. And this effort will promote peace in every other person—all 7.5 billion of them. What a legacy we can leave simply by deciding to express the smallest act of love! No friend or stranger will be left untouched.

CHAPTER 7

Choose Peace

"I choose peace instead of struggle." These six words are straightforward and strong—and yet, so simple. Yet all too often, they remain beyond our capacity to embrace, or perhaps even truly understand. We are confronted daily by situations and people we longingly wish we could control. For most of us, these situations no doubt arrive hundreds of times a week. I think that's the nature of the human condition. We want what we want when we want it. But "the wanting" is a waste of our spiritual resources.

Giving others control over what I thought or how I behaved was commonplace for much of my life. It began when I was a child, particularly in response to my dad, whose rage led to my own. Of course, I ultimately learned that fear was the culprit in both of our lives. But my willingness to allow others to trigger my thoughts—and, far too often, even my volatile responses—didn't end after leaving "the nest." Alas, it became even more pronounced.

Choosing a peaceful mind is now far more appealing to me in a moment of anger or frustration, or even a minor disappointment. My resistance to that choice lasted far too long. After all, we are constantly making choices, from what to wear or what to eat for lunch, to whom to call for a social engagement, to which job to apply for. For most of my life, it honestly never occurred to me that I could exchange the turmoil or confusion in my mind for peace. But having a peaceful state of mind has become far more interesting to me as I have grown spiritually—and as I have aged. Time is simply too short to give other people or the myriad situations confronting me rent-free space in my mind—a phrase I first heard more than a few decades ago in an Al-Anon meeting.

When I became a student of *A Course in Miracles*, my perspective on many things changed. Peace was one of the new, truly gratifying ideas I found in the Course. And this idea was reinforced on so many occasions by a kind man who was in one of my study groups many years ago. I can't say he was always at peace. On the contrary. Rather, it was his willingness to say, and thus remind the rest of us, that, regardless of what was happening in our lives, we could choose to experience peace that struck me. I believed him, wholeheartedly, and began to practice the idea. And my life did begin to change.

You're Not in Charge

Other than offering guidance to your children—who don't always follow it once they reach a certain age—you simply are not in charge of anyone or anything but your own perspective, your own decisions to think and behave in a certain way, and your own state of mind. Leave the rest to God.

Peace had never been a part of my own experience except when I went to visit my grandmother. She was soft and kind and always affirming. I loved visiting her. My own household never felt like Grandma's house. I became an overly anxious child as a result of the near-constant tension present in my home. Not surprisingly, I developed depression at a young age. Also, perhaps not surprisingly, I fantasized about disappearing. Of course, my condition went unrecognized and untreated for decades. Actually, I think my folks considered me "hard to handle," rather than legitimately troubled.

Those were different times, to be sure. I was born in 1939 and no one even talked about depression in the Forties and Fifties, when my struggle began to escalate. I had no idea what was wrong with me or how to talk about it. I just knew that I was uncomfortable everywhere, all of the time. And I was full of fear. I certainly had no one to talk to about it. In my house at that time, there were no soft shoulders to cry on. Everyone else was also troubled in one way or another.

The Sixties were famous for drugs, but not the kind that treated depression like my own. Although one drug that was actually used to treat tuberculosis was discovered to raise the moods of those who were taking it, there were no drugs hailed as answers to mental and emotional depression. Those of us who were depressed simply existed with it. And then I discovered alcohol!

My use of alcohol began at age thirteen. It became my drug of choice and seemed to provide a perfect coping mechanism. It did mask my feelings up to a point. Of course, it eventually worsened my condition. But I liked alcohol too much to give up using it. As is so often the case for those of us who ultimately get into recovery, alcohol finally turned on me and I sought help—but not until I had walked on the edge for many years. That I survived still amazes me. I do believe that Someone was watching over me.

Unfortunately, 12-Step programs were adamantly opposed to using any chemical for a condition like depression in the Seventies and Eighties, and I continued to suffer with bouts of severe depression until I was sixteen years sober. Regardless of the hard work I was doing in my recovery, and the few books I had already written for men and women in 12-Step programs, a peaceful mind, except on rare occasions, simply seemed beyond my capacity. A suicidal mind was a more common experience for me.

In fact, when I had been sober for about eighteen months, I was so deeply depressed that I developed a simple, straightforward plan to take my life. Enter Pat, and that aggressive knock at the door that changed my life. If Pat had not appeared on my doorstep, I'd not be sitting here writing these words today.

I was immediately uplifted by Pat's words of encouragement. She had also known depression and I trusted what she said. Even though my depression wasn't actually cured, I did experience a few hours of peace unlike anything I had ever known before. Pat convinced me that the abyss over which I hung was temporary—that all I had to do was reach for the hand of God, who was waiting on the other side. Pat, a complete "stranger," came into my life and left. And I remain to tell our story.

As is the case for alcoholism, there are myriad forms of treatment for depression, but seldom a long-term cure. Fortunately for me, I did finally agree to give medication a chance, even though I was leery of admitting it to others. Old attitudes die hard. Am I able to say that I experience a peace-filled mind every moment of my life now as the result of the medication? On the contrary. But I now have many tools to create that peaceful mind. Medication is only one of them.

Many of my friends and colleagues—probably not unlike those who surround you on a daily basis—experience tension and turmoil more often than they enjoy extended periods of peace. Those who meditate or are committed to a daily spiritual practice have a better chance of cultivating peace of mind. That peaceful state is, however, absolutely within the reach of all of us. It's truly as simple as making the decision to discard whatever has you in its grip to achieve the quiet of a peaceful moment. And that moment can, in time, become an hour, a day, and perhaps, for a very few, a lifetime.

Am I there yet? No. Do I expect ever to be there for more than a few hours at a time? Perhaps not. But what I have learned is that, in the blink of an eye, I can choose to see and feel peace instead of whatever person or situation has consumed my attention. A phrase I rely on every day—probably many times a day—is: "Help me see this (or her or him) differently." I can't explain how the shift in me occurs. I can only promise that it does. I instantly relax and have an unexplained, inner knowing that all is well. That I need not fret. That God is in charge and I can breathe easily. And peace descends like a soft blanket.

Having a peaceful state of mind has become far more interesting to me as I have grown spiritually—and as I have aged. Time is simply too short to give other people or the myriad situations confronting me what my fellow Al-Anon member called "rent-free space" in my mind.

Abe Lincoln once said, "You are as happy as you make up your mind to be." My experience suggests something similar,

You are as peaceful as you make up your mind to be. There is no magic to this idea. It's a choice, clear and simple. And it is one that will change how you experience your life every time you tell yourself to see things differently. To choose peace. God does the rest.

CHAPTER 8

Own Your Lessons

My lessons belong to me. *And your lessons belong to you.* Our lessons bear our names, and they will keep calling to us until we surrender to them. I am extremely fond of the idea that all the people we encounter on a daily basis—at work, in our neighborhoods, or even at meetings composed mostly of strangers—offer us the specific lessons we were born to experience. No one accidentally walks across our paths. I am equally fond of the idea that I can walk away from any lesson or person for which I don't feel prepared or to which I may perhaps feel resistant, knowing that the lesson will present itself again at a later time, maybe with the same person or maybe with someone entirely different.

Moreover, and this is a very important point, whomever you or I encounter has also *agreed* to the lesson. I consider that a real blessing, one that offers me relief and hope. It also eliminates a great deal of fear. I know that I will never walk through any lesson alone, because I and my learning partner both need it. We both agreed to it. *And* we can both walk away from it if we choose. Temporarily. The lesson won't forget us. We aren't discharged from it. It will visit again. I like to think of my lessons as waiting "in the wings" until I am ready to reconsider them.

I often think of another good friend when I consider this idea. He was a very learned Winnebago, head of the Indian Studies Department at a nearby university, who came into my life when I was doing work on Native American culture. At the perfect time, he became my mentor and friend. In time, he also became my lover. We drank and partied, and I nearly "went off the rails." By this time, my alcoholism was in full bloom. I do not doubt that his presence in my life was significant. In many ways, he served as my safety net.

This friend was the first male I didn't cling to. He was a free spirit. He was the first male I didn't try to control. His antics made me laugh. He was the first male to whom I felt equal and with whom I was truly comfortable. He was gentle and humble and totally accepting. From him, I learned what it meant to trust—myself and others—an experience .that prepared me for my present husband. My friendship with him superseded everything else in regard to our relationship. He could trust my loyalty, just as I trusted his.

I have learned that, when I accept all my lessons, how-ever they may have presented themselves over the years—and when I allow these lessons to shape how my life will continue to unfold—I can breathe pretty easily at this advanced age. I can review the past, like my experience with this man, noting how the impact of that encounter informed much of the rest of my life.

Not all past experiences are incorporated into the person I have become as gently as this encounter was, however. I am too often reminded of the really painful and confusing

20 Things I Know for Sure

experience I had as a young girl, when I was accosted and sexually abused by an older man on many occasions. In spite of the trauma I felt because of him, my spiritual development over the years has taught me that there was a lesson even within that recurring harrowing experience. And that has diminished its negative hold over my life.

I haven't forgotten the dread I felt whenever I was in my abuser's presence, but growing through these memories has helped me help other women who were also abused at some time in their past. It's imperative to consider that your lessons may sometimes only be for the benefit of others. You may experience something ugly so that you can walk another person through an equally ugly experience.

I'm not suggesting that the behavior of any predator is ever acceptable. On the contrary. But there is always something bigger in play—for both the abuser and the abused. This was certainly the case for me. And I think it's that larger context that we have to acknowledge. It's that context that serves us—we could even say enlightens us—as we grow spiritually.

I don't know what my abuser learned, and I actually don't care. But I learned about the power of forgiveness from the abuse, and time has shown me that forgiveness may be the most important lesson this life has to offer any of us. I believe this because any person we refuse to forgive, regardless of how grave or minor the offense, holds us hostage and prevents us from truly moving forward into our next necessary growth experience.

When we refuse to forgive, our growth is completely stunted, and this means that we can't help those learning partners we are *intentionally* meeting along the way either.

Remember, our experiences with all our counterparts have been "scheduled." And we agreed to them. In Myss' words, *we made the contracts.*

Never forget that every experience plays its part in who you become. It's the entirety of your experiences that creates the composite of the person you were born to be. This concept comforts me when I am confused over why something has happened, now or in the past. Neither my life nor yours develops willy-nilly. There is a perfect unfolding, a unique and perfect trajectory that fits each one of us. We can choose to put self-pity aside when the unexpected and seemingly unwanted happens. Being angry doesn't help either. There is clearly a reason for each of our experiences, although we may not understand it for years to come.

Here's an example. Just today, I visited a very good friend in the hospital. Thirteen nights ago, she woke up unable to breathe. Fortunately, her husband called 911. And for the last thirteen days, she has been in the ICU. For eleven of those days, she was sedated and on a respirator. She underwent a tracheotomy and is unable to speak because of the respirator. And she will spend many months in multiple therapeutic settings trying to regain all the aspects of her life.

I sat by her bed asking myself: What's the lesson here? I think it's too early to tell, but I'm certain of one thing: She will be grateful for every moment of life once this is in her past. Her condition gave me pause to consider just how quickly everything can change for any of us. And maybe her primary lesson is to remind the rest of us of how unpredictable life is. How fleeting our certainty that we can know just what to expect in any future moment.

Because this friend and I have known each other for forty-two years, I felt able to kid a bit with her and I promised her that she will understand the part this setback has played sometime down the line. She smiled and gave me a thumbs up. But I know the journey will be hard. And I know she knows that as well. If we knew what was coming around each next bend, we'd quite likely pull over to the side of the road and simply sit. But the future calls out to us and the lessons simply must be experienced. No matter what.

When my first husband walked out, I was devastated, in spite of the pain I had experienced throughout the twelve years of our relationship. His embarrassing alcoholic tirades and multiple infidelities should have sent me packing on many occasions, but I was too afraid of what my family would say. I was too afraid of being alone. I was too afraid that I wouldn't find another man. My codependency had gripped me so tightly that I simply had no strength or willingness to consider my own best interests. I mostly suffered in silence and, on occasion, prayed that he'd die.

How sad when I think of those days and the depth of my insecurity. Still suffering from the anxiety and depression that had troubled me so deeply since childhood, I was simply immobilized and couldn't do what any healthy woman would have done. However, because I have come to believe in the perfection of the evolution of our lives, I can now understand our hurtful "contract." I can even understand the role he was playing so perfectly in my life and actually be grateful for it.

My husband's departure sent me to the streets and my own alcoholic escapades, both with men I knew and with strangers. These escapades, many of them on the wrong side of town with the wrong people, eventually brought me to Alcoholic Anonymous and Al-Anon, exactly where I needed to be to become who I am today. He had played his part perfectly and so had I. And so had all the strangers who made their brief appearances. Not one of them was superfluous.

All Is Well

Believing, as I do, that you are always exactly where you need to be, having the experience you agreed to have, means that, no matter what comes your way, all will be well. All is *always* well.

This may be a new concept for you and you may find it difficult to believe at first. But lay aside your doubts for a moment and make a short list of some of the lessons you have learned—particularly those that have significantly influenced how you perceive life now on a daily basis. Then make a note of the people who shared these lessons with you. This exercise can help you discover the role and value of all you have experienced. It can quickly show you how each lesson, and every person who shared those lessons, led you into the next perfect experience.

Understanding that nothing and no one who crosses my path is superfluous to the journey that is mine to make quickly right-sizes me at those moments when I want to dig in and resist what lies before me. And even though I believe whole-heartedly in all I am sharing with you here, I am still quite capable of digging in. And I do. Too often. The fortunate thing is that every lesson that comes calling wears my name and will come again, and again, until I surrender to it. My resistance doesn't remove the lesson from my specific "classroom." What is mine to experience will wait for another time to pay me a visit.

I hope that you feel comforted by this idea. And relieved. If you allow it to penetrate your perspective, I assure you that it will give you a sense of well-being as you travel the path that is yours and only yours. And you will know that you are serving as a "learning partner" to those with whom you share your lessons. Never forget that each encounter offers both parties involved the next important lesson in the multitude of lessons that are specific to each of you. And these lessons were agreed to at another time and place, now long forgotten.

CHAPTER 9

Change Your Perspective

Your perspective is all that ever really needs to change. This was the message of my bestselling book, *Change Your Mind and Your Life Will Follow*, which explained in detail twelve simple principles for changing our lives. The primary point that I make in the book is that all growth results from our willingness to change our perspective—in other words, how we see the people or situations in our lives. The key word, of course, is *willingness*. Nothing changes if nothing changes, as the saying goes.

Willingness implies flexibility, of course, coupled with a readiness to change. It means accommodating others and being open to new ideas. Even more important, willingness can lead to abandoning our attempts to control others' opinions and behaviors. This is a big deal. The desire to control others in any way at all holds many of us hostage. And some of us live in this self-imposed prison most of our lives.

We are often convinced that our way of seeing any situation—*our* perspective—is the right way, the only way, to see what lies before us. But the willingness to let go of our obsession with how others see their own lives—even the same situation we are observing—is what promotes good will and peace of mind. Theirs and ours. We each have a perspective that seems valid to us and we must come to terms with that. And we simply will never know peace if our focus is on the perspective, the behavior, or the opinions of others rather than on our own lives.

Frankly, we have to monitor and be willing to change our perspective where necessary if new evidence presents itself. But it's never our prerogative to tell others what they need to do, new evidence or not. Never.

Many of you probably grew up as I did, far too "attached" to your circle of friends. I was always far too attached to whatever views people held as well, assuming that, in order to belong, I needed to share what everyone else thought. I feared that, if I thought differently, I would be "dropped" from the group. Sadly, at that time, I really had no personal perspective, no real sense of myself as worthy of a separate viewpoint. I had no voice. Whatever someone else's perspective was, I mimicked it. My security rested wholly in being and thinking as much like others as possible.

In my first marriage, I was thoroughly sick with codependency and insecurity. As a result, I tolerated hundreds of insidious situations. I also tried to figure out what my husband thought or believed about everything that came up for discussion, whether it was a news item, a book, or a movie. I wanted to mimic his every opinion because, in spite of his alcoholism and infidelities, he was a scholar and I considered him far smarter than I. I didn't want to be thought a fool; therefore, I wanted to match him thought for thought, perhaps hoping it would change him and save our marriage.

How far my life has come. Fortunately, I no longer need to think like you or like anyone else. Nor do I need to attach myself to your dreams and aspirations. I can celebrate your passions and not need to share them. However, I remain conflicted about my need to change how you see situations on occasion. My wish to "tweek" your perspective, which in turn changes your behavior (I hope), still has a stranglehold on me more often than I like to admit. Of course, I know that it's my perspective, not yours, that needs my attention, but old habits die hard. And every time I weaken and try to control another, I lose a little ground and destroy any peace of mind I was garnering.

I now recognize the insanity of my attempt to change other people, of course. I know it can't be done. But there is one person I *can* change: Me. That we try to do the impossible rather than what we can is the folly of the human condition. Trying to change the unchangeable has brought me nothing but frustration, sadness, and sometimes tears. And all the while, my own perspective waits for me to take control of it. Our perspectives don't resist our efforts to change, but it's not likely that we can permanently change them in one attempt. Just like old habits, old perspectives die hard. The two are intertwined, of course.

What does it really mean to change your perspective? How you see the world around you and all the people you encounter has developed over a lifetime. Thus changing your vision can feel like a monumental undertaking. It begins with a tiny decision. The pain of a current relationship or situation on the job or at home—perhaps with a friend or even a complete stranger—can be the catalyst that makes you decide that something needs to change. *And that something is always you!*

Actually, this realization immediately simplifies your life. Remember: No matter how hard we try or how clever our attempts, no one can ever change someone else. And throughout my many years of trying, I have come to appreciate that fact. If you or I had the power to change others in any way, we'd be beleaguered by the constant drain on our hearts and minds. Giving up the task frees us to live and experience solely what we were born to know.

Prayer for Change

I was helped many years ago by a quiet prayer that has had far-reaching implications for me: *Help me see this differently.* In other words: *God, help me to change my perspective and let go of my need to change others.* This subtle and simple idea has changed how I experience most situations that previously snagged my ego. Try using this prayer in your own life to open yourself up to new ideas that can lead you to peace rather than conflict.

The drive to change others is strong in all of us. And the freedom to choose to give up my attempts at control—attempts that are doomed anyway—has become far more interesting to me as I have aged. And easier too, I might add.

Here's an example. An acquaintance from one of my AA meetings and I were talking over breakfast about a current political controversy. Even though it's customary never to discuss politics at a meeting, the meeting was long over. So I expressed my utter dismay at a political situation that troubled me deeply. My friend's view on the subject was

20 Things I Know for Sure

completely different from mine, but I knew that to pursue the conversation further was inappropriate. So I simply turned to my trusty remedy and resolved to "see the situation differently." It was not that I was agreeing with him; it was just that I resolved to allow him to have his own perspective and to let the discussion move forward with another topic. I have learned that I can continue to like, even love, people who don't agree with me when I apply this simple remedy: *Help me see this differently*.

I want peace, inner peace and peace with all others whom I am destined to experience. Seeking to see them and the situations involving both of us differently when I am initially troubled gives my mind the peace it deserves. This opportunity is yours as well, of course. It's everyone's. And the more of us who choose to live by the simple words "Help me see this differently," the greater the chance for peace will become, within families, in neighborhoods, and between nations.

Isn't is amazing that five quiet words have the potential to change the world? But it's extremely important to know that it's not about looking for the change "out there." On the contrary, the change must first begin within me, and within you.

I well remember the first time, more than forty years ago, that I heard *The Peace Song*. I was at a Unity Church in Golden Valley, Minnesota. It was the closing song and the congregants stood, held hands, and sang it. The tears rolled down my cheeks. Because I had never heard the song before, the words moved me deeply, particularly the final phrase: "And peace begins with me." I left that morning knowing that I would come back the following Sunday. And that I had a new assignment to fulfill.

Taking responsibility for what is mine to do brings me back to where this chapter began. Changing your perspective can make the difference between having a stress-filled existence and a quietly peaceful one. Giving up the obsession to change others is where it all begins. And, as a matter of fact, it's where it all ends as well.

CHAPTER 10

Hear the Voice of Spirit

There are two voices in our minds—the ego's and the Holy Spirit's. I treasure the simplicity of this idea. It helps me determine which voice is guiding me. And it reveals which voice everyone else is hearing as well. If what I am about to do or say, or even think, is anything unkind, then I know that I have allowed the ego to take charge of my mind. Of course, the ego does speak loudest. And it speaks first. And it always leads us in the wrong direction. But alas, we listen to it anyway and create dissension where none need be. Again and again.

I was introduced to this concept of two voices in *A Course in Miracles* and it became a principle that I rely on daily. I think it quite clearly "separates the wheat from the chaff," as the saying goes. We know which voice a friend, a family member, or even a total stranger has been listening to as soon as we hear their words or observe their actions. Nor can we pretend that we aren't controlled by the ego's voice if we are feeling embarrassed or ashamed of our own behavior in any way.

I appreciate simple, straightforward ideas like this one. Perhaps even more so as I have grown older. Trying to analyze what lies behind someone's words or behavior no longer interests me. What I hear or see generally speaks volumes, and I can usually tell in an instant if the person I'm observing is being held hostage by the ego. Moreover, I can recognize that this is still often the case with me. And I can also recognize when I am listening to the soft, kind, and loving voice of the Holy Spirit, the voice I seek to hear but too often allow to be drowned out.

Fortunately, each one of us can choose to monitor what we are about to say or do by simply pausing for just a moment before responding to another person or to any situation. It's amazing how many times in a day a simple pause—just a of couple seconds, actually—has prevented me from causing harm. And it's unfortunate how many times I have failed to pause for that moment and then felt immediate regret.

Just the other day, I was on the phone with our cable service company. There was a rather large discrepancy between the bill and what I thought I owed. I asked to speak to a "higher up" and was told that no one was available. I was pretty upset and thought that I was being lied to. I made a few comments about their company and what I felt I deserved after having been a customer for more than twenty years. And then I hung up, but not without an expletive. I felt both ashamed and embarrassed—both for having let this situation get out of hand and for allowing my ego free rein.

In this situation, the wrong voice had held me tight in its grip. And I knew the incident would trouble me all day unless I addressed it. So I made another call to the company, hoping to get the same representative, but doubting that would happen. Indeed, it didn't. So I asked to speak to a supervisor about a billing matter and one came on the line. I explained my previous call and the outrage I had felt, and made my apology. The supervisor was extremely nice. She accepted my apology on behalf of the representative I had confronted earlier and made an adjustment to our bill. I was surprised, to say the least. But—and this is more important—I was also so glad to be free of the shame I felt over my behavior. Doing the right thing, for the right reason, can result in unexpected "gifts." In this instance, it certainly did.

We can't take back our words. Likewise, our actions are always visible. I think it's helpful, particularly at the end of the day—or even earlier, as in the example just described— to assess where we fell short of our better selves honestly. It is by making amends where necessary that we learn to serve humanity better the next day. And making amends is an effective way to begin the process of eliminating old, bad habits, which, in the final analysis, are actually only evidence of letting the ego run our lives.

Here's another example of my ego at work—one I'm not proud of, but that makes my point. When my husband and I first began living together, neither one of us listened to the softer voice that would have helped our relationship. We were both insecure and afraid of rejection, but also afraid of losing ourselves in the relationship. I had been married before, very unsuccessfully. Joe had never been married. He had never intended to marry, in fact. Our relationship didn't look like "a match made in heaven." We were both ego-driven, to say the least.

Shortly after I moved in, we built a screened-in porch on the back of our house, one we intended to share. We had drawn an imaginary line down the middle to designate our personal space. On my side was a hammock. It was where I retreated for quiet time and to meditate. On Joe's side was a large table where he did his art projects.

One day, I went out to the porch and sensed that he had moved his table slightly into my space. I expressed my annoyance. He reacted angrily to my accusation, of course. In the blink of an eye, with absolutely no prior thought, I swiped a completed work made of small mosaic tiles onto the floor, a project he had been working on for weeks. He was apoplectic.

Joe raced upstairs into my study where I was writing my dissertation. He pulled open all my file cabinets and tossed their contents onto the floor. Papers and course files were everywhere. And cancelled checks galore. I ran upstairs with a camera and photographed the mess, insisting I was going to show his mother what he had done. There we were—two individuals completely held hostage by their egos. And the result was total insanity.

We each became very quiet, knowing that our relationship might well be over. Neither of us spoke. We both retreated from the scene. A couple of hours later, we reluctantly sat down at the kitchen table to assess the damage. Neither of us really wanted to walk away, nor did we want to take all the blame. There was plenty to go around. Amends were made—not entirely willingly perhaps, but we moved on. We were both a bit skittish at first and on high alert. The good news is that this happened nearly forty years ago and we are still together.

Was it the last time that the ego's voice held us hostage? On the contrary. It has intervened probably hundreds of times during our years together. Remember, the ego always leads us down a path of destruction. However, we have both learned how to access the voice of the Holy Spirit more

20 Things I Know for Sure

willingly—a voice that is always present. And we have both learned the *intentional* value of our relationship. Moreover, we both know the wonderful payoff that comes from listening to the softer voice. Peace is a gift—inner peace and a peaceful relationship. Peace is guaranteed to everyone of us when we allow the Holy Spirit to guide us.

The Gift of Peace

What a blessing to know that living in peace is as available as your willingness to seek it through the choices you make. And serving as a peaceful example to all those others on your path—never accidentally—is a key part of the journey that is yours to celebrate.

When I was younger, I drove myself crazy wondering what my journey was all about. It took sobriety, the willingness to seek the guidance of others and my Higher Power, and the sometimes daily decision to lay aside my disbelief that there was a perfect outcome for every experience I was having. Now I know my own effort is all I need to handle. God has the rest.

My life has gotten so much easier with the advancing years because of a few principles by which I now try to live:

- I have given up trying to control what's not mine to control, most of the time.

- I have given years of practice to listening to the softer voice of the Holy Spirit and much (though not all) of my behavior has changed.

- I know that I can change my perspective on any situation and there will be an instant, visceral shift in how I feel.

- I know that there are no accidents, that whatever comes my way was and will always be a lesson intended for me and there will be spiritual growth within it.

- I can recognize appeals for healing and help, and—more important—I know exactly how to respond to them.

We are very lucky travelers on this journey. We will never end up where we shouldn't be. And we will always have a very willing guide to lead us peacefully where we need to go. There really isn't anything more that we could want. Is there?

CHAPTER 11

Heed Your Fellow Travelers

Those who share our journey are our teachers, *everyone of them*. I consider this a profoundly stunning statement, one I have grown to appreciate greatly over the years. When I first heard it from an acquaintance in a 12-Step group more than forty years ago, I scoffed, to put it mildly. I could see how a parent, a sibling, or a significant relationship partner might have had something important to teach me. And surely the many educators I experienced from grade school through graduate school were teachers of significance. But all those ordinary and sometimes disquieting travelers I encountered along the way? Were they really teachers too? I strongly doubted that. In fact, in a few instances, I felt repelled by the thought of it.

In time, however, I became willing to reconsider my resistance. Through the work of many people of renown and great intellect who also believed this theory, I became convinced that I should at least consider it. Why not assume that everyone is a teacher who has a part to play in my evolution?

And why not let those recollections inform my journey to see where they take me?

What has been helpful for me—and what may be equally helpful to you—was to make a list of the individuals who have crossed my path from childhood on who tugged at my memory. They were tugging for a reason, I thought. Think of this list as a "timeline" of sorts—one that takes note of the people you have encountered and how your interactions with them affected you, taught you, changed you. Consider how they changed your outlook in particular. Some may have inspired you to explore a new interest, a new skill, even a new talent. Others may have taught you what to avoid—what not to do, to be more blunt. Each made his or her mark, absolutely. And revisiting these experiences offers you a worthy history lesson that can help explain who you have become.

When I think back to my childhood, I remember certain grade-school friends who impacted my life in both good and not-so-good ways. For instance, a classmate I met in first grade who lived three blocks away from me was chubby and had pigtails. She was an only child and had more of everything than I did. Way more. This was in the Forties, the heyday of movie magazines, and she had subscriptions to many of them by the time we were in fourth grade. I had none. And she always bragged about all she knew regarding what "the stars" were doing, as if that really mattered. Unfortunately, to me it did.

By the time I was nine, I already felt ignorant and envious of this girl. Then I started to notice that her parents were seldom there at mealtime. She was basically spoiled, but not really happy, and her behavior reflected it. I didn't have a perfect childhood by any means; in fact, it was fraught with tension. But I never doubted that my parents would be there at mealtime and to say goodnight, even though no one "tucked me in."

Unfortunately, my interactions with this classmate made me guarded and insecure around other kids. I feared being taunted for not knowing something they knew. I became self-conscious because of her. And that feeling of low self-esteem followed me for years. I surely can't blame her for all my feelings of inadequacy. Many experiences unrelated to her contributed to them. But whenever and from whomever the seed of low esteem is planted, it continues to grow until a perceptual shift occurs. And that shift didn't happen in my life until I was convinced there was a Presence protecting me. And that didn't happen until I was in my forties.

Reviewing the past for what it can reveal about our teachers throughout our lives is enlightening, to say the least. On occasion, it can also be disturbing, because not every teacher may have had what appeared to be our best interests at heart. But I have gratefully come to believe that each one of my fellow travelers made his or her entrance on cue and that I ultimately grew from each encounter, no matter how difficult it may have been at the time.

I even learned from the sexual abuse I experienced as a child. I was afraid to tell others about it and even felt inexplicably responsible for it. I was afraid I'd be blamed for it. Worst of all, I didn't think my parents would actually believe me, because the predator was a family member. That period of my life was very difficult, but eventually I gained a different perspective on the abuse and was even able to see the abuser as a teacher who ultimately inspired me to embrace forgiveness. I didn't get there easily or all that quickly, but I got there. And the willingness to forgive him has enriched my life beyond measure. I'm doubtful that any lesser experience could have done that.

Moreover, I have found that I can share what I learned about forgiveness with others who find forgiveness to be a stumbling block. And I have also been able to talk with many about the abuse and how it fit into the bigger picture of my life. Because I'm no longer held hostage by it, I have served as an example to other women, showing them that they can get free as well. I consider these my most important moments as a teacher, in fact.

Here's another of my experiences that may trigger a recollection for you and help you build your own list of teachers. It involves a boss I had while working in the sportswear section of a department store in the mid-Fifties. I was still in high school and I loved working "downtown." I was promoted very quickly from stock "girl" to salesperson. And I was good. My boss took note of that and encouraged me to pursue merchandising when I went to college. He had high hopes for me and, even though he was bearish on occasion, he often praised me in his own way. From him, I learned to trust myself. I gained confidence. And I dared to offer ideas and opinions about our department's prospects for success with certain items of clothing. My ideas impressed him. I had never felt that kind of approval before, even from my parents.

To this day, I am grateful to this teacher. I learned the value of praise from him, not as manipulation, but as an important way of honoring another person's value in the moment and, ultimately, to the universe at large. This lesson has influenced my thinking as well as my behavior for decades.

Another boss I had many years later was also bearish to all of his underlings. Much to my surprise, however, he promoted me on more than one occasion and, when I became manager of a major department in our company, he was amazed at how "improved" his former employees became. When he asked how I had done it, I answered: "Praise." He seemed disconcerted. I'm certain he had never considered the value of praise before. I surely had never received it from him in a direct way. In fact, he often left me nasty notes about the work my department had done and signed the note with a skull and crossbones.

I am so grateful to my first boss for honoring me as he did so I could pass on to others what he taught me. And I'm confident that's the primary reason we interact with others throughout our journeys. It's not simply so we can learn something, but also so we can help to educate others who join us on our paths seeking exactly what we can pass on. We are teachers as well as students, and those we *intentionally* meet will serve others as we have served them. It is a never-ending cycle of give and take.

My recollections are very important to me because I want to appreciate just how far I have come and, even more, be able to pay quiet homage to all those individuals who helped me get here. I'm sure I'd not be where I am now if I had not been in the company of so many instrumental teachers throughout my lifetime. Have you recalled one or two of your own teachers by now? Here is another of mine that may help you—the woman who welcomed me into the doctoral program I completed at the University of Minnesota.

I was full of fear when I decided to go on to graduate school. I was newly separated from my husband of twelve years, and only decided on graduate school because I could see no other avenue for moving forward. I knew I wasn't a scholar like my husband, but I was naive enough to try something besides teaching second grade.

When I knocked on her open door, this woman smiled and invited me to sit down. She knew who my husband was, but we didn't discuss him. This was about me and her gentleness convinced me that she saw possibility in me. She helped me look at the daunting curriculum, assuring me that I could handle all that would be expected of me. Her belief in me, a young woman she didn't actually know, was all I needed. The first course on the agenda was hers and I walked out of her office with a sense that I really could succeed, scholar or not.

That was a turning point for me. I discovered in graduate school that I could write effortlessly, a skill very few of my classmates possessed. And I have been writing ever since. I certainly didn't know at that time that my life's work would be as a writer, but the stars aligned for me. I got into recovery for my alcoholism and found myself in the right place at the right time to write the first daily meditation book for women in recovery. This fellow traveler had played her part, as did every professor I encountered throughout my course of study. I wrote for all of them and each, in turn, heaped praise on me.

Moving Forward

You never get to where you end up all on your own. You are helped every step of the way. Not all "help" may register as positive—either at the time or in your recollections—but every experience moves you forward on your specific journey. And that's what's important in the final analysis—to move forward. You are constantly moving forward. And until your last breath, you will meet the teachers you agree to encounter.

My advancing years haven't diminished the power of this experience for me. I know that my lessons will continue. And my role as teacher will continue as well. Just yesterday I had a chance to pass on what I had learned about forgiveness to a young woman who is recovering from exceedingly vile sexual abuse. It's not easy, or even appropriate, in a situation like that to say, "Just forgive the perpetrators." But when I share how forgiveness has freed me from my own memories and allowed me to move forward, I know that I am discharging my role as a teacher.

Passing on to others what we have learned grounds us and strengthens our own spiritual understanding, our own acceptance of the way our encounters have created the tapestries of our lives. I believe, without a shadow of a doubt, that every experience I have had from childhood on contributed to my becoming an alcoholic, and that belief has led me to write more than two dozen books. Every difficult person, every harrowing experience, every success, and the many failures I experienced have added to the brilliance of my particular tapestry. And how pleased I feel with that realization.

I hope by now that you have also come to appreciate the lessons you have shared with the many individuals whom you have met by design. You found each other in the right way, and at the right time. Our lives unfold perfectly. Even when they feel most uncomfortable, there is perfection at play. There is perfection. And all is well.

CHAPTER 12

Seek Oneness

The ego is separate; Spirit is One. The choice to be separate and sit in judgment of everyone is the trademark of the ego. It's my opinion that, from a spiritual perspective, the ego really isn't our friend. It may be true, as many psychiatrists and psychologists say, that as youngsters we need to develop a healthy ego in order to find our place in the family and among our peers. As we mature, however, we need to understand how to harness the ego for good or it can lead us astray. And when that happens, the ego's role as a troublemaker can be fed by our willingness—some would say our desire—to see others as adversaries, individually and collectively.

All we really have to do is watch the evening news to see evidence of angry egos run amuck—in communities, between countries, and among opposing cultures. We can't experience peace of mind, even a hint of it, when we look at anyone, whether an acquaintance or a complete stranger, as an "enemy." What makes so many of us choose to live in perpetual turmoil? Why can't we calm the voice that drives us to be spiteful, mistrustful, judgmental, or far worse? Or can we?

Remember: The ego always speaks first; it always speaks loudest; and it's always wrong. Moreover, it *never* suggests that we be kind or loving. But the voice of Spirit is its opposite in every way. And we have to be vigilant—extremely focused, in fact—if we want to hear that voice. The good news is that the voice of Spirit never leaves us. It waits patiently to be heard. No matter how long it may take, it quietly waits to help us be our better selves.

Moment by moment, we choose the kind of experiences we will have. And from my perspective, that's extremely empowering. No one can decide for me, or for you, what kind of day or what particular experiences we are going to have. No one. Even when we are bombarded by the nagging voices of naysayers, we are in charge of our own thoughts and deeds. We are the choice-makers.

As I write this, I'm reminded of a passage in a book I read many decades ago. This passage enlightened me far beyond any idea I had encountered prior to that moment and I still hold it very dear. The book, written by a Jesuit priest named John Powell, was *Why Am I Afraid to Tell You Who I Am?* In the book, Powell relates an experience he had while strolling with a friend down a New York street. His friend was a well-known journalist and they made their usual stop at the newspaper vendor by his friend's apartment. The vendor was always rude. Powell's friend was always kind and invariably gave the man a tip, even though he was never thanked.

Finally, after observing this exchange on far too many occasions, John asked his friend why he was always so kind to a man who was "so undeserving." His answer stunned me: "Why should I let him decide what kind of day I am going to have?" Instead of seeing the man as a jerk who deserved to be rebuffed, his friend simply responded in a loving way,

20 Things I Know for Sure

obviously listening to that quieter voice to which we all have access—the voice that isn't spiteful; the voice that doesn't pass judgment; the voice that doesn't instigate harm where none need be. Powell's friend's response served as a powerful example of "joining with" rather than "separating from" a fellow traveler.

At that point in my own journey through life, and well beyond that point as well, I had allowed myself to be held hostage by what everyone else was saying or doing. And if I wasn't the loving center of every other person's attention, I was devastated. I'm embarrassed to admit that I clung to my companions in search of undying acceptance and even devotion. To say I was sickly codependent is an understatement. My life was nothing if others weren't focused in a loving way on me.

I had absolutely no idea then that I was making a spiritual journey on which I would be given multiple opportunities to allow others to be who they were, and learn in the process that I was healthy and whole without anyone's approval. That idea was definitely not on my radar screen. In fact, unfortunately, that realization was a long time coming.

The spiritual journey, as I have come to embrace it now, is truly and simply about joining with my fellow travelers who are on my path by design. And it has become my intent, each day, to be aware of the Spirit within them rather than the ego. You can't glimpse anyone's Spirit if you are listening to your own ego as it screams judgmental thoughts about the person standing before you.

Ego thoughts don't even have to be hideously ugly for them to be wrong. Even just a silent snicker about a person's clothes or hair, or perhaps an opinion someone recently expressed, means that my ego is holding me hostage—

which, of course, means I have said "no" to joining that particular soul on his or her journey. More specifically, it means I have said "no" to the primary reason our paths crossed in the first place.

Any unkind thought, whether expressed out loud or silently, separates me from a sister or brother. It's the acknowledgment of our Oneness, of our shared Spirit, that heals us, all of us, in time. And that opportunity for healing is the sole reason we have encountered one another. I have come to believe that, beyond just joining with our companions on this journey we all are making, we must learn to see ourselves as necessary beings comprising the One. As is expressed in so many spiritual tracts, God is incomplete if any one of us is missing. The One, the Whole, is comprised of the collective of which we are all, individually, a part.

The decision to pause and remember why we are here every moment is really pretty simple, and it's the same decision for each one of us. There is nothing mysterious about it at all. It's simply choosing to *join* by being the extension of peace in every encounter, which is inherently an expression of love as well. The moment we allow the ego to be in control of, first, our thoughts and, then, our actions, we cause the world to grieve just a tiny bit more.

I believe wholeheartedly that we are each responsible for the world we all share, whether that world is full of grief or full of joy. Our thoughts and our actions are ultimately felt everywhere, by everyone. What we do or say to one is transferred to all, whether we live in Minnesota or Bangladesh.

This idea is analogous to meteorologist Edward Lorenz's theory of the "butterfly effect." Lorenz postulated in the 1960s that small weather changes at one place can have a major impact elsewhere. For instance, a storm in Indiana can be the catalyst for a hurricane in the Bahamas. To look at this another way, one that I find more understandable, Lorenz said that the small wings of a butterfly send out a vibration that is infinite and that can ultimately cause a tornado. From this, we can infer that nothing that occurs anywhere happens in total isolation. Everything affects everything else. There is always a ripple effect. And the interconnectedness of every occurrence and every person in the world around us should give us reason to pause before thinking any thought or taking any action. Wouldn't you agree?

The Ripple Effect

There is a vibrational effect that is registered when any thought is shared with the universe. Thus it follows that good thoughts inspire other good thoughts. Likewise, loving actions inspire loving actions. Unfortunately, mean-spirited thoughts and actions also inspire mean-spirited thoughts and actions. It's up to you to choose which you will put out into the world.

If we accept this theory, it follows that the effects of what you and I think and do are awesome. They are ultimately, *and always,* reflected in what a person in another part of the world may choose to do. This should make all of us alert to every thought we have and every action we take. Let's never forget that what the ego is pushing us to do can have devastating effects. We are constantly impacting others, not only here and now, but everywhere else as well. It's obvious, isn't it, that, under these circumstances, listening to the quieter, loving voice of Spirit for direction is a far better choice?

I used to think this idea was farfetched, albeit interesting. But now it pleases me, because it makes everyone of us responsible for the kind of experiences we will personally have, as well as the experiences we are nurturing in the universe from which others can benefit.

The theory of the 100th monkey, which originated in 1952 on the island of Koshima, also supports the importance of this idea. Researchers who were feeding sweet potatoes to a group of monkeys observed that one monkey invariably washed the sand from its sweet potato. The monkey's mother observed this behavior and mimicked it. In time, all mother monkeys and their children were following the practice. And then, quite surprisingly, the practice appeared on other islands as well—islands far removed from Koshima. The researchers postulated that a critical mass had been reached on the first island that shifted the perception, or practice, of all primates everywhere.

It's my theory that every opportunity we take to benefit another soul in a loving way can help to develop a critical mass that can shift the universe in a profoundly comforting way—one that heals the concerns of every living person. Why not consider the possibility that what is true for primates, weather phenomenon, and the fluttering of butterfly wings could also be true for humankind?

And even if these theories aren't strictly analogous from a scientific standpoint, doesn't it make sense to be comforting and kind anyway? Doesn't it make sense to follow the simple suggestion that Mother Teresa made so many years ago? Be kind to everyone and start with the person standing next to you.

The ego doesn't have to be in charge of our thoughts and actions. We can, with persistence, say no to that incessant voice. The trademark of the ego is to be separate, not joined with anyone, and to sit in judgment always. We can make another choice. There is another voice that is waiting for us to hear it. Why not now? Why not be part of the change that can lovingly shift the direction of the universe? Why not choose Oneness?

CHAPTER 13

Strive to Be
Truly Helpful

We are here only to be truly helpful. Can any more direct statement be made about our purpose here in this classroom of life? And can we be given any simpler assignment? I think not. All it requires of us is the willingness—some even say only a *little* willingness—to consider what is needed in the moment when we are face to face with one of our fellow travelers.

To be truly helpful absolutely rules out unnecessary criticism. It also rules out mean-spirited judgments. And it definitely rules out dismissing another person as undeserving of our next opportunity for compassion. Remember: *There are no accidents.* Those you meet on this journey you meet by design—a design that wears both your own name and the names of those you enounter. And every encounter is a holy invitation for the expression of love.

I'm thrilled that our purpose here is simply to be helpful. It eliminates all the hemming and hawing that we so often do when confronted with an unfamiliar or unwelcome situation.

There is never more than one choice to make. Never. For instance, the person who rudely pushes ahead of you in line at the grocery store is merely presenting you with an opportunity to be your better self. It's not always easy to rise above your inclination to say something you may regret, but you can. And indeed, in that particular moment, with your mind coupled with your attitude, you will be all the better for it.

Being helpful wears many faces. It can be as easy as smiling. Or giving a quiet nod in the direction of the person crossing your path. Or maybe it means listening for the tenth time to the tribulations of a friend full of self-pity, or perhaps giving your attention to a complete stranger who seems in difficult straits. One of the most common opportunities to be helpful is just answering the phone when a friend or an acquaintance calls.

To be honest, we don't always want to make ourselves available by answering the phone. And there is no rule saying we must. However, if you have an inner, niggling feeling that you should, even though you'd rather watch the end of a show on television, or finish reading a chapter in a great book, I think we can consider that the nudge is coming from the God of your understanding. Your friend's need is actually offering God the opportunity to speak through you to him or her. If this idea seems a bit far-fetched to you, think again. Each one of us is here as a vessel through which God's words can be revealed to those who seek them. But our "little" willingness is necessary.

What I quite often realize in situations like this is that what I say to my friend is exactly what I'm in need of remembering at that moment as well. Being truly helpful to ourselves, as well as to someone else, is the real gift of this principle. Remember: What we do to (or for) one, we do to (or for) all. Our expressions of helpfulness know no bounds. The recipients are everyone, everywhere.

I think this principle could even be considered a bit self-ish, because I have realized on probably thousands of occasions in my eighty years that, when I have chosen to be help-ful, my own spirit is lifted. Making a kind or loving gesture changes how I feel internally, quite quickly. And if I make this gesture when I am not feeling particularly loving or kind, it very quickly right-sizes me. My attitude is adjusted in a nanosecond. More important, making the gesture allows me to make an important difference in someone else's life. And then I experience the difference as well.

There isn't anything earth-shattering about this idea. It's really just common sense, as are all twenty of the principles presented in this book. But we so often fail to implement the common-sense ideas that can change lives, particularly our own.

This idea puts me in mind of Fred Rogers, the star of a children's television show that ran for thirty-one seasons during the Sixties, a time of great turmoil in our country. The show's purpose was to reach children with a message of love, a message that was certainly counter to the multitude of violent images of the Vietnam War that were shown in every home every night on TV news. Rogers, an ordained Presbyterian minister, was a kind and very gentle man who quite simply wanted children to feel loved and accepted just as they are. He wanted them to know they didn't need to do anything special to receive the love they deserved. He chose to "minister" to children as his life's work and was determined to do so.

The show was an instant success. Children loved Mr. Rogers. They instinctively recognized his warmth and sincerity. The show was simple in every way. Hand puppets expressed messages about being thoughtful and kind and the children were mesmerized. The puppets talked about serious subjects too, like assassinations and war. After watching a documentary about his life recently, I was struck by how much we need this message again, not just in the media, but in our families, in our communities, and particularly in politics and on the world stage. The idea of affirming people as they are has been lost. Praising rather than criticizing has been lost. Seeking to be silent rather than loudly judging someone else has lost its appeal as well.

We all suffer from this malady, unfortunately. I'm not immune to it either. Pointing at others and saying "It's them, but not me" is oh, so wrong. It's all of us, frankly. I'm as guilty of condemning rather than affirming others as the people I judge, who are simply condemning more publicly. Whether we condemn openly for all to hear or simply harbor the condemnation in the recesses of our minds, the damage is done. When we condemn, we're not being truly helpful. And every time we fail to be helpful, we are hurting, not just those close at hand, but ourselves, along with more than 7.5 billion other people as well. That fact should give us reason to pause.

But we can change. That's the good news. And no matter how incremental our change may be initially, it's a beginning. When Fred Rogers introduced the idea for his children's show so many years ago, no one was particularly excited about it. In fact, he eventually had to go before Congress to make a case for funding for public television. His quiet passion for helping small children to feel loved and accepted is what swayed a very resistant committee to release 20 million dollars to PBS. *The Mr. Rogers Show* became a reality solely because of Fred's ability to persuade.

Small Steps

Your own passion for doing the gentle, kind thing can sway the mindset of the people around you. And it's an accumulation of small steps taken by ordinary people that, in time, will change the mindset of this world we share. I'm convinced that a critical mass will be reached. Maybe not in my lifetime, and maybe not in yours. But in the *right time*. Everything does have its time. Let's not forget that.

Each one of us sits in a position of power. At every intersection of life, we have the opportunity to make a difference that can change the moment for the person we are about to meet as well as for ourselves. And the ripple effect of our meeting is as unending as the ripples that spread out from the toss of a flat rock across a peaceful lake.

Changing the circumstances of how we all experience any part of any day is the best opportunity any one of us has upon awaking each morning. As I've said already, life isn't complicated. Our decisions about how to handle each situation aren't complicated either. The choice is the same every time. Be helpful or turn away. The payoff for being helpful is a glorious one. If you haven't made it a practice to choose this response at every opportunity, you are simply cheating yourself out of a chance to make each day joyful. You will get back what you offer, so offer kindness.

We are here only to be truly helpful. The moment is now. Not next week when you go on vacation. Not when you get that hoped-for raise. Not when the neighbor you abhor moves away. Now. There is no better moment. Actually, there is *only* this moment. What a blessing this moment will be for you and for me if we make the choice to be truly helpful every time someone, friend or foe, crosses our paths. Lending our voices to the critical mass puts us in harmony with a choir worth joining.

CHAPTER 14

Embrace Forgiveness

Forgiveness is the key to a life peacefully lived. This sounds so simple, doesn't it? And yet, if it were, far more people would be living contentedly peaceful lives that would lead to greater peace in our families, in the workplace, in our communities, and even between countries throughout the world. From the looks of things, however—particularly if the nightly news or the twenty-four-hour cable news cycle are any indication—there is nothing simple about the attainment of peace. And it appears as if the number of people who possess a gentle, peaceful state of mind is actually on the wane.

Perhaps we aren't really sure how to get to that peaceful state. I believe that forgiveness will take us there, but I'm guessing that not enough of us know what forgiveness looks like or what it feels like. And it is quite possible that to forgive in a given situation may seem unfair. After all, the harm was done, wasn't it? Isn't an apology in order first?

I'm not sure I can explain how you can learn to forgive, but I can share what I have learned about the look and feel of forgiveness, an exercise that I have practiced for many years now since becoming willing to change my life. The decision to make that change is something I'm grateful for every single day.

Forgiveness didn't come naturally to me. On the contrary. I was the proud queen of grudges for many years, which completely prevented me from experiencing even a hint of peace. I grew up in a family where holding a grudge was as commonplace as gossiping about the neighbor who had multiple late-night visitors.

If your "emotional toes" are stepped on by someone, either accidentally or intentionally, you have a right to harbor a grudge. My parents were constant role models in this, unfortunately. They criticized each other incessantly, which all too often led to holding grudges. I'm inclined to say that one or the other was resentful on a daily basis. Family meals were nearly always very tense gatherings because of some grudge one parent was holding against the other. We kids never knew how to navigate around the tension. I often left the table complaining of a stomach ache.

Our household was not a warm, fuzzy environment. And by the age of eight, I had learned first-hand what holding a grudge could do for me. It could keep people away or make them feel badly. Perhaps of even greater value, grudge-holding allowed me to feel superior, which was, of course, a total sham. I actually felt inferior to nearly everyone, all the time—everyone.

How sad it makes me, even today, to remember how separate the six of us in my family were. My mom and dad never talked lovingly to each other, at least not within ear-shot of us kids. And my siblings and I kept our distance too, from them and from each other. I wasn't necessarily resentful of my sisters and brother, but neither did I feel closely connected to them. We were a household of very separate individuals, never seeking comfort where we didn't expect to find it.

The only familial comfort I recall receiving as a child came in the arms of my maternal grandmother. She was the embodiment of love. She almost made up for what was lacking in my home. Almost. But the two weeks every summer I stayed with her and my granddad were always a welcome reprieve. The evening carousel rides at the nearby park, followed by a stop at the Frozen Custard, certainly made every peaceful day even better. How sad I felt every July when my two weeks with them came to an end.

In all honesty, I rather doubt that my family was all that different from many families in those times. Growing up in the Forties and Fifties meant lean times for families like mine. My parents had lived through the Depression and all six of us had experienced the uncertainties of World War II and the Korean conflict. Food and gas rations were normal as well as necessary. A freshly killed pig from my uncle's farm hanging in our cellar meant we'd at least have meat for a while.

How well I remember the startling buzzer at school that meant we needed to duck under our desks quickly for protection, just in case a bomb fell—and the air raid sirens in the evenings and the blinds that were quickly pulled throughout our house so "the enemy" wouldn't detect the lights in our homes.

I think living through those tense times made it all too easy to be very nervous and unnecessarily suspicious of others, which led to being standoffish. I personally think it made holding a grudge far easier as well.

Fortunately for me, getting into 12-Step recovery, first with Al-Anon and then with AA, opened the door to learning what forgiveness can offer—the release it promised, the opportunity it nurtured to join with others, the pathway to emotional healing it fostered. I must admit that the gifts forgiveness could offer had never entered my mind prior to 1974. I was hanging on tight to every grudge and every resentment I had ever developed over the first thirty-five years of my life. I figured that I had a right to each and every one of them. I was a victim, after all!

My introduction to forgiveness actually came from a minister with whom I shared my first 4th and 5th Steps. He was a kind man who never once interrupted me as I read all seventy-eight pages of recriminations—"he did this" and "she did that." Only after I'd finished did he speak. In a quiet voice, he said, "You really never looked at your part in any experience." I was devastated. I had failed the exam! But what he said next was truly eye-opening: "Perhaps it is time to forgive those you *think* have injured you." I had never considered forgiving those culprits. They had hurt me, after all, and seeing my part in that experience simply wasn't yet on my horizon.

Fortunately, my level of discontent made me a willing "student." I observed how others I had grown to respect were changing, and I didn't want to be left behind. I wanted to be like them. I desperately wanted to belong. I tried to imitate their behaviors and share their beliefs. I did my best, in fact.

And then, three or four years later, I experienced an epiphany. I was introduced to *A Course in Miracles* and learned about a path to which I'm still committed on a daily basis. I am grateful to the Course, as I am to the 12 Steps, for introducing me to forgiveness in a way that made sense to me. This new information enhanced my willingness to forgive and my journey began to change quite significantly.

In the 12 Steps, I learned that forgiveness would allow me to let go and move forward. In the Course, I learned that I had to forgive, not only others, but myself for my judgments of them. Next, I learned that forgiveness could close the separation between myself and others and erase that awful sense of distance that I abhorred. The Course taught me about being joined, *as One*, in the human community. And this idea gave me what had been missing from my life since childhood—a true sense of well-being and belonging.

The Gift that Keeps on Giving

Forgiveness is one of those gifts that keeps on giving. Because your heart is lightened, you simply become softer and easier around all the people who gather close by—all the individuals who have been drawn to you by design, both theirs and yours. And remember: Even those you find it necessary to forgive have played a very important role in your divine journey.

I had felt separate, different, quite alone for my entire life. And now I had hope that I could experience what belonging really felt like. However, I had work to do. Lots of it. I had to be willing to forgive completely to get there. And not just selectively.

I have come to believe, after years of practice, that we must make forgiveness absolute. We must forgive everyone. Anyone we hold outside the sacred circle of forgiveness prevents us from being at peace. Anyone. I know that's a strong statement—some might say a very tall order—but it's key. As far as I'm concerned, we will never arrive at that place of quiet contentment that I want to inhabit if we don't follow this suggestion completely.

Is this an easy assignment? Not at all. I wasn't so easily convinced that forgiving my first husband for his many transgressions and infidelities was going to benefit me in any way. After all, he didn't even know I was going through the act of forgiving him. But my heart was lifted by the exercise. I no longer felt "tied" to him through my anger. I no longer felt that the marriage still had me in its grip. When we allow those we aren't willing to forgive to hold us hostage, we are crippled by our inaction. Moreover, our relationships with all others are hindered by our unwillingness to let go of past hurts.

The biggest struggle for me in my search for peace was in forgiving the person who had sexually abused me as a very young girl. I hadn't even reached puberty. I was confused and scared and trapped. And I felt I had no one to talk to. I was stunned into silence, actually, and my connection to my parents was so fraught with uneasiness that I didn't feel comfortable telling them what was happening to me. I simply tried to avoid him at family gatherings, often unsuccessfully. I felt I clearly had had no part to play in this drama, so forgiving him—and myself as well for my judgment of him—seemed grossly inappropriate. But I was being held hostage. And something needed to change.

I am so grateful for the willingness to which I finally surrendered. That willingness allowed me to forgive and to discover peace in a profound way. I have not forgotten just how relieved I felt when I let that hurt and resentment go. He never knew I forgave him, of course, but I knew. And my heart felt lighter. Every relationship felt more honest. And I was aware, in a fervent way, that my forgiveness had freed me, and him as well.

Remember: There are no accidents. Whomever you encounter appears right on cue. And regardless of the experience you share, there is a reason for it. Perhaps you won't understand the reason for many years, but it will have played its part in your life—even those experiences that you have to wrestle with later in life. Fortunately, we are never left to wrestle with any experience or memory alone. As a dear friend of mine says so quietly, so often: God is always working things out. And that is a promise we can take to the bank!

CHAPTER 15

Sit Quietly

God is always working things out. When my friend shared this simple idea with our group at an AA meeting, it really wasn't new to me. There are no new ideas, are there? But it was the way she said it that really caught my attention that night. Her voice was quiet, but unwavering. Full of certainty. It had provided her great strength, she said, during a very troubled time.

I had been sitting there that night feeling great uncertainty about how to handle a troubling situation with an acquaintance—a situation that felt very sticky and untenable. My friend's words reminded me who was in charge, who was working it out. And I was finally able to breathe, to let go and move on, trusting in the God of my understanding to handle what clearly wasn't mine to resolve. I left that meeting feeling a lightness I had not felt for days.

When I look back over the eighty years of my life, I can enumerate literally thousands of instances when God did work out situations that were troubling me. Fretting for a time before simply getting tired and letting go is not all that unusual for most of us, unfortunately. I'm pretty sure that many of us function this way. It isn't our natural inclination, at the first sign of discontent, to say: "This one is for you, God." Many of us eventually get there, but I would love to get there before the handwringing begins. Wouldn't you?

I have thoroughly loved reviewing my past and fondly recalling specific times when God stepped in, working out a situation that was too big for me to handle—for instance, when Pat knocked on my door just as I was about to turn on the gas and end my life. It helps me remember that God will always step in. I simply have to be willing to "step aside" and open my door to make it possible for everything to change. It's one of my most deeply held spiritual beliefs that angels always hover around us "on assignment," so to speak. Pat was surely on assignment as my hovering angel that fateful day or I wouldn't be here writing these words today.

Remembering those times when God came to call has also helped me in my role as a mentor, and in some instances as an AA sponsor. Sharing with others what has been true in my own life experiences is so often exactly what someone who is struggling to believe needs to hear. And just as often, it's what I need to remember as well. I don't think we can recall those miraculous moments when God came to call too often. If you ever have reason to doubt His Presence, simply take a few short minutes to make a list of the times in your own life when He was with you. He was there. Again and again.

I'm now even inclined to say that perhaps some of my past experiences occurred precisely so that I could authentically come to the aid of someone else troubled by something similar. Helping ourselves and someone else at the same time is one of God's many miracles, I think. There are no accidents. What I need to experience in the moment I will experience. Those I need to help in the moment will undoubtedly be present as well.

One thing I'm very certain of as I review my life is that God was never unavailable. *And God will never be unavailable.* I just have to step aside once I have put forth whatever effort is required of me. I'm guessing that's the stumbling block for many of us—knowing where our effort ends and God's work begins. Until we let go, God can't step in. But God won't leave our side. He will wait patiently until we step aside. I know that instinctively, as well as experientially.

When I first got into recovery, I heard the phrase: You are only in charge of the effort; God's in charge of the outcome. Although I didn't really understand this, I liked the sound of it for a long time before ever trying to put it into practice. It seemed simple, straightforward, and manageable. Kind of like the slogans that hang on recovery room walls: "Let Go and Let God;" "One Day at a Time;" "Easy Does It;" "Keep It Simple."

The first time I read these slogans, I scoffed. They seemed ridiculous, unattainable, and far too simplistic for the likes of me. But the passage of time can certainly influence how we think. Fortunately. Now I savor the slogans. Every one of them. They are my shorthand to a peaceful moment. Knowing that, if I sit quietly, God will work things out relieves me, changing my total demeanor in a mere moment.

Life need not be so difficult, so full of stress. And I'd have to say that, as I have aged, I've become far more willing to seek the simpler solution to life's problems. Letting things be, for instance, reminds me that God is working them out, (whatever "they" are). Maybe this is a typical response for a person getting along in years. I'd like to think that we do get wiser with age. I think we also simply have less energy to fight battles that don't even need our attention. I'm often reminded of a saying I heard in Al-Anon many years ago: We don't have to join every argument we are invited to.

The ability to evaluate what's important and what's not is a gift we grow into. And it's one that frees me from so much angst. Deciding that most "troubles" can be shelved for another day, or ignored completely because they don't really matter in the larger context of our lives, is like breathing fresh air after having been cooped up in a dirty old attic all day. I have often heard it said that the more you focus on a problem, the bigger it gets. Doesn't it make sense that the opposite is also true?

Open Your Mind

You can't "hear or see" the solution to a problem if your mind isn't quietly open to the possibilities that are always there—possibilities that are trying to reach you through that inner voice I call God. You are never left to handle any situation alone. God is always present within and ready with His solution if only you are willing to open your mind and hear it.

Our lives, though sometimes very painful because of specific teaching moments, are really never beyond the reach of the steady hand of God, who is always walking beside us. We never walk alone. Never. Those near misses when you were driving drunk in the wrong lane or when you stepped off a curb without looking and a car slammed on its brakes were not just "lucky misses." They were quite intentional misses integral to the work you are here to accomplish. And God was on duty to help you. As always.

Take a moment to review your life and to savor a few of those specific experiences where God was present. In the very moment of a "near miss," we don't always pay homage to God. We simply think we were lucky, once again. However, I truly no longer believe that luck plays any role in our lives. Anything anyone refers to as luck is actually the hand of a Higher Power who had a better idea for that life in that particular moment. We can't count on luck. We *can* count on God.

Just sit quietly; God is working things out. Isn't that a wonderfully comforting notion? And it's not just a platitude. It's true. The happenings in my own life, and in yours no doubt as well, prove it. Take a few moments, here and now, to bring to mind one significant memory where God took over.

Perhaps my sharing another example from my own life will trigger a memory for you. When I finished my dissertation, the six professors who made up my committee were all given a copy of it. Five of them read it and approved it enthusiastically, but the sixth kept putting me off. The date for my final oral exam had already been set, so I went to his office and expressed my concern about the delay. He said the timing wasn't his problem, but he did agree, although not eagerly, to meet with me the next day.

The following day, I arrived at his office and, without even looking up from his desk, he said: "This has to be completely rewritten." I was stunned into silence. He was talking about a full year's work. When the shock wore off, the terror set in. What was I to do? I had a mere three weeks before my oral. There was no time for a rewrite. And then I said, much to my amazement: "Can we go through it so you can share your concerns?" He wasn't happy about it, but he agreed. *And then the miracle happened.*

For three hours, he pointed out his objections and I responded to each one. I truly wasn't even conscious of his words or mine. And yet we talked. It unfolded like a dream sequence. It felt as if I were having an out-of-body experience. At the end of our conversation, he looked up and smiled (for the very first time), handing over my dissertation after signing his name. "Terrific," he said. "I'm satisfied. You pass."

I walked out of his office as stunned as I had been when he first said the document had to be completely rewritten. I walked down the hall, found a pay phone, and called my husband. "You won't believe what just happened. God made an appearance and did for me what I couldn't have done myself."

Just as my friend reminded me so many years later, all it takes is our willingness to sit quietly. Even for just a moment. That's all the invitation God needs to work things out as they need to be worked out. I needed to complete that degree because it would open the door to the rest of my life—a life that has included many books, including this one. There is an order to the events of our lives, and God is in charge of that order. How lucky that makes us.

I'm convinced that our recollections help us to see more quickly when it's time to step aside so that God can come to our aid. Solving our own problems, or trying to, becomes habitual and most often leads to failure. But there is never failure when we allow God to work things out. All we have to do is sit quietly. The solution will present itself. Quite perfectly.

CHAPTER 16

Cultivate Loving Thoughts

It's our thoughts that cause us pain, but we are in charge of those thoughts. This idea makes us wholly responsible for every feeling—the good ones as well as the bad ones—that we have, because it's our thoughts that trigger them. We may not always cherish this idea. Indeed, our thoughts, especially when they are held hostage by the ego, often take us back to painful memories. They also frequently exaggerate something uncomfortable that may just have transpired. And all too often, they negatively anticipate future happenings and exacerbate any dread we may be feeling.

Our thoughts can obviously injure us, but they can also injure others when the ego has commandeered them. Just this morning, at my AA meeting, the topic centered on how our minds tell us crazy things that we believe and then act on. If we willingly allow our minds to be controlled by the ego, we will hear nothing worth listening to. Ever. *Nothing!*

However, our thoughts can be wholly positive if we just listen to the Holy Spirit. This may not happen as frequently, but it can become far more frequent if we are willing to be more vigilant about the "meandering" of our minds.

Thoughts don't just "happen" willy-nilly. We create them. And whether we put the ego or the Holy Spirit in charge of them determines the very nature of every single experience we have. Actually, that's the upside of this principle. We don't have to live in constant dread or pain about anything, past or present. *You can change any thought you have with a simple, on-the-spot decision.* You have the ability to choose the voice you want to put in charge of your thoughts, and thus your life.

You Have the Power

You have the power to determine how you navigate through each day. The ego works overtime to make you forget how to be thoughtful, kind, and positive. But you just can't afford to let it take over, which is exactly what it's primed to do. Moment by moment, day in and day out, that is its intent. You have to reclaim that power by choosing to listen to the voice of Spirit rather than the clamorings of your ego.

Making the decision to change a thought may seem a bit mysterious. Thoughts seem simply to "appear" in our minds quite unbidden by us, don't they? But that's not what actually happens. On the contrary, we are selective about which voice we choose to hear—the ego's or the Holy Spirit's. And that choice, in turn, gives birth to each and every thought we have. Of course, that sets the stage for all our actions as well.

As we saw in chapter 10, the voice we choose to hear defines not only the tenor of each day we are going to experience, but each encounter as well. And this is key: Neither voice has the power to hold us hostage against our will. But the ego, because of its demanding assertiveness, *can* hold us hostage if we don't empower ourselves to make the choice to express love and kindness.

How often do you honestly "observe" your thoughts and then evaluate them? I'm guessing this may not be one of your regular habits. It probably isn't for most of us. And there is no shame in that. Thoughts come and go. Most of them seem innocuous, and often they are. And yet, specific thoughts can lead us astray, taking us where we don't really want to go.

For instance, a judgmental thought about an acquaintance can lead to nothing positive. Savoring this thought obviously poisons any encounter with that person. In all honesty, it poisons every encounter you may have with anyone else as well, unless you are vigilant about letting go of the judgment—not always an easy thing to do. Far too often, we love to hang on to judgments because they make us feel superior for a time. And then they begin to eat at us. Fortunately.

It is extremely common not to pay very much attention to our thoughts, because most of them are fleeting. And this undermines our attention to the ones that linger, ultimately causing us and others harm. Politics is one area that commonly trips people up in this way—myself included, more often than I care to admit. Any candidate or pundit who opposes my opinion always seems worthy of my judgment. But when we get hooked by the ego into making judgments like this—whether we express them or not—we lose our peace of mind. Our negative thoughts have us in their control. We don't even have to express these thoughts to be burned by them. Ouch!

Here's another example of how the ego can steal my peace of mind. I have a neighbor who exerts very little control over her dogs and her young children. Many of us on the street are concerned about the safety of both the kids and the dogs because drivers don't expect to find them darting across the street at will. Many of us have gently suggested to this neighbor that her children and dogs are in danger of being hit because cars travel fast on our street. She seems oblivious to our concerns.

I'm gobsmacked, actually. It's not my business, I know. But the children are extremely vulnerable and their mother appears too busy with her cares inside the house to pay attention to what's going on outside.

My ego has a heyday when I get involved in situations like this one. It creates one negative thought after another, and then dwells on them. After focusing on these thoughts for a time, I'm often inclined to share them with someone else, adding unnecessary fuel to an already simmering fire in my mind. Being a party to this kind of gossip helps no one. Not the kids, not the dogs, not my neighbors, and not me. But my ego loves to create chaos and takes advantage of any opportunity I give it. And then peace, once again, escapes me.

Turning our minds—and thus all our thoughts—over to the ego rather than to the Holy Spirit is a habit. And that means the pain we create for ourselves is habitual as well. If we want freedom from this pain—whether it be emotional, mental, or even physical—we have to take charge of where we put our attention, instead of letting a bad habit rule the moment. So often, I put my attention where it should never be.

I balked at the idea that I could actually impact "the reality" of physical pain when I was first introduced to this idea. But not anymore. I have come to believe that physical pain is like all pain. It's kept "alive" by my paying attention to it. When I am involved in an activity that claims my full attention, whatever physical pain I was experiencing dissipates.

For example, I lived with debilitating head and neck pain for many years. However, I was always vaguely aware that, when I was working on a book or speaking at a conference, I was oblivious to the pain. It took me a long time to realize that being absorbed by an activity that I love, one that gets my full focus, pulls my attention away from pain, and that, in turn, controls my awareness of it.

This same realization has been true for the past two years, during which I have suffered from severe hip and knee pain. And even though I did finally give in and replace both joints, I was always aware that, when sitting at the computer writing or while in a great conversation with a friend, I felt free of the debilitating pain. This proves to me that when my mind is anyplace other than on whatever pain is troubling me, it's barely even noticeable.

Our thoughts can exacerbate our pain. Clear and simple. I have thus come to believe that we can "cure," or at the very least lessen, any pain we have created with our thoughts by simply changing our minds. My experience has made it obvious to me that pain of any kind is only as real as my willingness to keep it alive and in the forefront of my mind.

The awareness that no thought is in charge of us, that actually the reverse is emphatically true, empowers us and changes everything about who we are and who we can become. All I have to do is revisit the trajectory of my life to see multiple examples of this.

As a child and well into my adult years, I felt that I was "less" than everyone else. Not as cute. Not as smart. Not as destined for success as everyone else. My mind was unknowingly imprisoned by my ego, and that fact never even caught my attention. Indeed, it was completely lost on me. Then recovery from addictions cracked the wall of my resistance to a new idea.

And how grateful I am for the education I have been blessed with through the 12 Steps of Alcoholics Anonymous, as well as the enlightenment I received thirty years ago when I embraced the spiritual path presented in *A Course in Miracles*. I shudder at the thought of where my life would be today without these two pathways to peace. There is simply no doubt that I'd still be vying for attention and struggling to fit in, occasionally entertaining the thought of suicide— something that was all too common with me.

I can't claim that I "have it all together" at this ripe old age of eighty, but I am at peace more often than not. And I have decided that being at peace quite often is nearly as good as enjoying constant peace. Too much of any one state of mind just might cause me to lose my edge, after all.

CHAPTER 17

Pause . . .

Hmmm. This single word, these five letters, may just be the solution to nearly every uncomfortable situation any one of us encounters. Can it really be as simple as that? Just pause? Well, there are many things we can do within that pause, of course. We can count to five. Or ten, if we need more time for composure. We can make the proverbial plea to our Higher Power: "Help me see this differently." We can seek to see the other person who has "rattled" our serenity as Spirit, regardless of who he or she is. And we can remember that every encounter is either a loving experience or a call for healing and help.

When we do the latter, a simple pause can make us aware of a call for healing and help. This call can take many forms, some of which may throw us completely off guard—for instance, an unexpected angry outburst from a total stranger. But a call for help can also be as quiet as a very tearful young woman or child standing on a street corner. Either call can be met in exactly the same way—with a pause followed by a prayer asking for guidance regarding how to respond.

It's helpful to remember, particularly when confronted by an angry outburst, that even though you may doubt it, you are always in the right place at the right time whenever you encounter another person, whether it be that angry stranger or that tearful child. You have both agreed to meet for the next lesson you were each born to experience.

Unfortunately, many lessons are harsh, while others tear at our heart strings. And yet, we never face any of them without the help of our Higher Power, who is always available to guide us to embrace each and every experience with a loving and forgiving heart.

A simple pause can effectively relieve us of the impulse to overreact to any person or situation that has gotten our attention. And the impulse to overreact is a far too common occurrence for many of us. Although I have curbed this impulse somewhat, it still beckons to me, rather insistently, when I am confronted by something or someone who quickly gets under my skin. Even when what I encounter is a mild invitation to get involved, I have a history of stepping over the boundary into other people's space. When this happens, I realize I'm once again "back to the drawing board" of life. Thank goodness we are allowed "do-overs" as we continue this journey, the only one that is quite specifically ours to make.

I'd like to be able to say that I'm entirely free of the impulse to overreact. After all, I'm in my eighth decade of life. But my ego still takes control far too often, and it's always the ego that pushes me—and you as well—to react rather than to, quietly and consciously, take a moment to consider a proper action, *or none at all*. Reaching the point where I can take no action at all is my current goal.

20 Things I Know for Sure

Be Vigilant

The ego sets you up to overreact almost before you know what has hit you. Remember: It always speaks first and loudest. Therefore, you must be vigilant and resist its call. If my own experience is any indication, I'd have to say that your vigilance must be almost continuous if you don't want to let the ego run your life. Never doubt that that is its intent. Day in and day out. Experience by experience. Moment by moment. So be vigilant.

Pausing to allow the Holy Spirit time to offer you a better idea about how to respond in the moment is a skill you can practice and perfect—a skill that can change the tenor of your life. The Holy Spirit can give you access to a built-in pause button that can make all the difference in how you see what lies directly before you. With the help of Spirit, everything takes on a softness that it didn't have when viewed only through the eyes of the ego. There are always two ways to see any person or situation. Simply pausing can open the door to always seeing things in a gentler way.

How I wish I had been introduced to the simple idea of pausing before responding much earlier in my life. I'm convinced it would have saved me from thousands of unnecessary conflicts—with my dad, with my ex-husband, with my siblings, and with my mother as well. Even my present husband has far too often been on the receiving end of an overreaction he didn't deserve. The ego simply never chooses to remain in the shadows. And we tend to shed far too much light on it, thus allowing it to make too many decisions for us. Simply pausing just isn't part of its formula for living.

The good news for all of us is that making the decision to pause before taking any action, even before making any sound, isn't difficult. It's nothing more than a new habit. And a very good one at that. In one respect, pausing is like performing a tiny meditation, like taking a very brief "vacation" from the overly active ego. The freedom this offers us can be addictive in a good way. Doesn't that sound like a sane invitation to change?

I can't pretend that I always remember to take advantage of this simple technique. But it feels so good when I do. Staying out of other people's business, regardless of what kind of business it is, is like taking a breath of truly fresh air. I used to be guilty of making everyone's business my business. I saw it as being "helpful." Then, an Al-Anon friend shared that very significant thought that I mentioned before, and that I have tried to live by ever since: There are two kinds of business; my business and none of my business. The choice is simple. Isn't it?

For some readers, the clear and simple value of just pausing may seem too simplistic an idea for solving life's myriad problems. I'm not so sure I could have appreciated it earlier in my journey. Before, I was all about rushing to solve problems, whether they were mine or not. I was certain that my value was tied to being constantly available—actually, more like being constantly necessary—to the needs of others.

Maturity, coupled with 12-Step recovery and the wisdom that's inherent within this blueprint for living, has changed how I view nearly every part of my life, and thus your life too. My problems are solely mine to solve. And yours are for you alone to solve. And if I need to pause to discern if a problem is mine or yours, it's certainly doubtful that it's mine!

Becoming a model for others by making the choice to pause before reacting is a worthy example of how to live with greater peace. And we do watch others, don't we? We learn from good examples as well as bad examples. Being a good example may be the very trigger that changes how another person begins to live his or her own life. When you pause before responding to any experience, you enjoy such a freeing and empowering feeling. Not being controlled by the antics of anyone or any situation opens the door to a far more peaceful life.

I'm ready for that more peaceful life. Aren't you? Being willing to pause at every opportunity before making a response—to any situation and to every person, regardless of what that experience looks like—can change us for the better. But it can also add more than that moment's peaceful benefit to the universe that encompasses all of us. We are an interconnected body of humans, all 7.5 billion of us. And what we do in one instance is registered within every moment lived by everyone.

Let's pay careful attention to what we are doing and who we are becoming. It's not just for ourselves that we live, that we pause, that we act. Always be conscious of your importance to the life that pulses throughout this universe we all share. And may our journeys be gentle—always.

CHAPTER 18

Journey with God

The idea of journeying with God was completely foreign to me during my youth. If I had been introduced to it earlier in my life and embraced it, I think my journey would have looked considerably different. As a youngster, I didn't connect with God at all. My family didn't attend church regularly, although we kids were dropped off at Sunday School on occasion. As an adult, I suspected that was when my parents had sex. In high school, I did attend a church youth group, but irregularly and primarily for the social advantages.

At big family gatherings, grace was skipped unless my drunken uncle managed to weasel in a long, meandering prayer. His devotion to the Bible was generally part and parcel of his drinking escapades, possibly to draw attention away from them. Unsuccessfully, I might add.

I truly never considered the absence of God in our family life as either good or bad. It was simply the way it was. No one ever stood over me reciting the Lord's Prayer when I went to bed. I think I must have learned "Now I lay me down to sleep . . ." at a friend's house while sleeping over.

My next-door neighbor was a girl my age who went to a Catholic school. I remember feeling jealous that she had a rosary to lead her in prayer. I told my mom that I wanted to be a Catholic so I could have a rosary. "Wait until you are older," she said. In the meantime, however, my neighbor taught me how to say the rosary. I was thrilled, but still didn't ever pray for real.

I don't know if believing in a caring God would have alleviated my near-constant fears about life in general when I was a young girl, but I'm inclined to think it could have made a difference. I was anxious most of the time. I well remember Sunday afternoons when I was in the second grade. I was always sick to my stomach, often to the point of vomiting, because of my fear about school the next day and my teacher, who terrified me.

Many Sunday nights, I woke up my mom because my stomach hurt so badly that I couldn't lie still. My interruption of their sleep enraged my dad. My mom took me to see a doctor and he said she shouldn't worry. I simply had a nervous stomach.

My second-grade teacher didn't like me for some reason, and she often poked the top of my head with a pencil—which hurt. I dreaded every time she walked down the aisle in my direction. I begged my parents to take me out of her class, but both the principal and my dad thought I needed to stay put.

It was a very painful year and, midway through it, my appendix ruptured. To this day, I've wondered if I brought all that on as my way to escape that teacher's pencil point, if only for a few weeks. And possibly to make my dad feel guilty as well for not hearing my anguish over being in her classroom.

Because I had come home from school sick on so many occasions that year, I was told in no uncertain terms that I couldn't do it again. But the day I ended up in the hospital, I ran home in so much pain that I couldn't lie still on the couch. My mother called the doctor and he rushed me to the hospital in his car. I was taken into surgery immediately. My dad sat by my bed after the operation with tears in his eyes, sorry for not believing how sick I really was. I still hated my teacher, but I felt vindicated. And I was glad my dad felt badly.

Could trusting in a caring God have changed any of this? Who can say? But many of the less significant things over which I worried throughout my young life might have been alleviated. For instance, I was always in doubt about my friendships. I lived in fear that I would be left out when someone planned a big event. And I was sometimes, but probably not intentionally. At that time, I had no idea that my life had been divinely orchestrated and that God was my constant companion no matter where I went.

Revisiting my past, as I am wont to do, I can now see the perfect pattern of the events in my life—the happy times as well as the sad ones. I can also see how my first husband's infidelities and the sexual abuse I experienced as a young girl contributed to the person I was becoming. All of these memories give me reason to pause, with an understanding for which I am so grateful. Each and every experience played its necessary part in my development. To be able to celebrate this fact gives me great satisfaction.

Along for the Ride

Every situation, person, and experience you encounter contributes to where you are at this very moment, and God has been along for the entire ride. To be more correct, He's been driving the bus. And He will continue to drive the bus. And you will continue to be His passenger until your ride is over. That awareness can give you so much pleasure and bring you so much pure peace.

I don't think my parents or my eldest sister ever believed in the constant presence of a God who understood their needs and provided for them. My sister talked often about her inability to believe that there was anything after death. Fear and anxiety ruled their lives. This makes me sad for them. Still. And I hope that, by now, they can see that God actually was present in every moment of their lives. Nothing they did was ever "out of sight" of a loving God. We don't have to know that for it to be true.

I have an inkling that we take who we are at the time of death to *our next experience.* Only then can we see, with new eyes, what we did not realize while on our previous life's journey. Of course, I can't know if this is true, but it gives me solace, and comfort is what I long for in what remains of my life.

Even though I believe in a Presence that guides me—and I'm confident that millions of people share my belief—there are probably nearly as many who never feel the comfort of a caring guide. Some may reject the idea outright; others may simply do so because they feel no pull in that direction. I am not sure this idea would ever have captured my imagination without my journey into alcoholism and drug addiction—a journey that was scripted quite perfectly for me, and one that led me into the recovery rooms where I "met God."

Whenever I have a moment of doubt regarding an upcoming engagement, my relief is swift and sure when I review, even cursorily, the events from my past. Whom I met, where I was led—and both in the context of what I experienced—all fits perfectly into the tapestry that has been mine to weave. Not one thread has been extraneous to the whole. This gives me assurance that nothing about the future will be extraneous either. Wherever I am called to be and whomever I meet there are on my "calendar of events" even before I open it to review the upcoming day.

The comfort of knowing that *all will be well*, as English theologian Julian of Norwich told us hundreds of years ago, is music to my ears and feels like a hug around my beating heart. Neither you nor I need fret about anything. That we do fret is purely the work of the ego—that incessant, very loud voice that only survives because of the attention we give it. Its very existence is directly tied to our insecurities, which it works hard to create and then keep alive. Without them, the ego's power diminishes, thus allowing us greater freedom to choose the "other" voice.

The phrase "all will be well" has a potency to it that is life-changing if we allow it to permeate our existence. It surely comforts me like a warm blanket on a very cold night. It is true simply because we are not in charge of our lives, or anyone else's either. We are traveling a specific path that is divinely directed. We will never be confronted by a circumstance "accidentally."

Whatever situation calls to you is on the agenda that bears your name—an agenda that you share with the God of your understanding. So lay your concerns aside. Now and forevermore. What will be, will be. Amen.

CHAPTER 19

Forget About
Being Right

Would I rather be peaceful or right? For far too many of us, this question poses a conundrum. Actually, my struggle is that I want to be both peaceful and right at the same time. And occasionally, that's even a possibility, but those times are few and far between. Being agitated or discontent in even a minor way is more the norm for many of us, I think. Coming to appreciate the blessing of peace first requires that we be willing to seek peace—and then be patient. It also requires that we actually choose peace over any other option that calls to us moment by moment—and there are many of those options to choose from.

The two voices in your mind are key here. One voice—the one that always speaks first and loudest—will never cultivate a peaceful mind. It will never encourage anything resembling a desire for peace within you. Nor will it inspire you to respond lovingly toward anyone. Of course, I'm referring to the ego's voice, which insists that you be ready to "fight." It pushes you to demand that you are right, regardless of the situation, the conversation, or the encounter you are experiencing. While the ego engages your attention, you will never experience the peace that is always available.

Fortunately, there is another voice that, in each moment, quietly awaits your awareness of it. This voice will never fail to help you choose peace. All you have to do is surrender to its quiet, unending presence in your mind, and peace will be your reward. Spirit places no timeline on your willingness to honor it. It is simply there, in each moment, waiting for you to surrender to it.

When we take careful note of the many others on our path, we can discern, ever so quickly, which voice has gotten each traveler's attention. This is true whether we are at work, at home, in the grocery store, or in a line of traffic going from one calendar commitment to the next. A person's behavior— the honking horn, the snarky retort, the angry stare—always reveals the voice that's being honored. Not surprisingly, we are surrounded every day by people who are quite insistent that they are right. And if that's the stance we take as well, no resolution or forward movement can occur.

How fortunate it is that we have been introduced to the idea that there is "another way" to navigate our journeys through life. I never experienced that "other way" in my family of origin. There was one "right" way to see or behave in every situation, and it was my dad's way. As the rebel in our family, I dared to argue with my dad about nearly every stance he took and every opinion he voiced. I simply wanted my own view of things, right or wrong, to be heard. And I didn't want him to decide for me or my siblings or my mother what we should think. I was quite convinced I was doing a service for my family. I wasn't.

I have acquired at least some wisdom with age. For many decades, I was pretty certain that being "right" was necessary to my well-being. It took several 12-Step recovery programs for me to lessen my grip on being right, as well as immersion in the principles of *A Course in Miracles*. And it took the experience of leading hundreds of workshops and writing more than two dozen books for me to surrender fully to the gift of choosing peace over insisting that I was right. I was stubborn. Now I am grateful.

Peace Begins with You

Choosing peace over the need to be right can change every aspect of your individual life. And it also dramatically impacts all the relationships you experience—which means each relationship partner is freed from your demand to be right as well. The idea that peace begins with you has no boundaries. Every single time you make the choice to be peaceful rather than argumentative, or worse, you send forth a peaceful ripple that flows unendingly until everyone is touched. *Everyone!*

Knowing that each of us individually, and all of us collectively, can choose peace by making a very simple decision sounds too easy, doesn't it? After all, we live in a world that is in constant turmoil. Tuning in to the evening news is all the proof we need to confirm this. Full-blown wars are being fought in multiple locations and refugees are fleeing their homes with no refuge in sight. Chemical poisonings, starvation, and ethnic cleansings make the ultimate attainment of peace seem very unlikely for some people, now and for years to come. Unfortunately, these aren't the only examples of the true heartache that is being felt by so many.

And yet, *and yet*, making the choice to extend the hand of peace in even the most mundane situation is a beginning! A tiny, very powerful beginning. One person to another person, on a street corner, in a meeting at work, over the dinner table at home. Any of these simple situations can be an opportunity to sow the seed of peace. The attainment of peace—anytime, anywhere—rests solely in the hands of those who truly believe that peace, now, is the greater choice, as long as we are willing to honor it.

Choosing peace is the obvious solution to every ill that affects any of us. It's not a mysterious choice. Nor is it elusive. It's as close to you as your next thought, which usually precedes your next action. What this means, in this next moment, is that each one of you reading this must consider the possibility that you can make a difference—not only in your own life, but in the lives of many others as well. What a noble choice this is. And so very doable.

All of the ills that we can point to around the globe, *all of them*, are the direct result of someone in power insisting that he or she is right about some circumstance that is having dire consequences for all those who have less power than they do, or no power at all. This is not a new scenario. Human history is replete with examples of situations in which someone's power over millions, or even tens of millions, of others has resulted in unspeakable crimes against humanity.

But dwelling on the horrors of the past, or on those that exist right now, immobilizes us, thus preventing us from saying and doing the next right thing for ourselves and for those who need our right choice in this moment. In a way, we live in fortunate times, because the media doesn't let atrocities go undetected. I'm not suggesting that being bombarded by bad news is good for our psyches, but it does allow us to choose more consciously where we should and can make a difference.

I am so grateful for the education I have received from 12-Step programs and the Course over these many decades, because my entire perspective on life's lessons and possibilities has changed. I know now that my journey has always been purposeful. I know now that no person I encountered was an "accidental traveler" on my path. And I know now that my work here is still ongoing. My job isn't done. Nor is yours. Your very awareness of these words that I have written and that you are reading is proof of that.

Let's consider what this means. I think it means that we are being called to attention. We are being summoned to step forward and do our part in making this world a far more peaceful place, not just for ourselves—absolutely not just for ourselves—but for the billions of souls who inhabit this planet. I know this probably sounds like a grandiose, even outlandish, plan for the likes of you and me. But if not us, who? It requires so little, really.

You don't have to move to somewhere new. You don't have to take a new job or leave a relationship. You don't need any special education. Nor do you need to read any particular book. You only need a little willingness—a tiny bit of willingness, actually—to consider being kind in the next moment. To be kind is the easiest way to cultivate peace within a relationship, thus within a family, and then within a community. Remember the ripple effect. A kind word is like a stone that's tossed in a quiet lake, sending ripples out to others from its peaceful center.

Choosing to be peaceful over insisting that we are right, *even in those cases when we may be right*, is an honorable choice that promotes the well-being of all those who are present—

and even those who aren't present as well. I have known the inner struggle of making this choice in my own life. I learned at the feet of a master the "necessity" of being right. I also eventually learned that pushing my agenda brought no peace of mind, to me or to anyone else. No relationship was ever enhanced by my behavior when I insisted on being right rather than choosing peace. On the contrary, many were destroyed.

So would I rather be peaceful or right? At times—after all these many years of seeking the kinder, more peaceful approach—I still itch to argue, insisting that I know best. And sometimes I give in to that itch! I am still a work in progress. At age eighty, I still need to practice making the right choice.

One of the truisms that I learned in Al-Anon has been of great help. When in a disagreement with a friend, a spouse, or even a stranger, the best response is to say: "You may be right." When I remember to do this, the tension of the moment is immediately lifted and all parties can breathe quietly.

Be not discouraged if you fail, again and again, in your attempts to choose the peaceful journey—the one that consists of moment after moment making the right choice. Even your failed attempts move you closer to peace. And this world will be changed through the process of people making one successful attempt after another. Just like raising a child, it takes a village, multiplied many times over, to create a world where we are all allowed the gift of living peacefully. All that is asked of us is to be one tiny, beating heart in the process.

CHAPTER 20

Just Let Go

I have never heard a simpler, more comforting suggestion in my more than forty-five years of recovery than "just let go." The first time I remember hearing it was from my first sponsor in Alcoholics Anonymous. I was whining incessantly, which had become my pattern, about a relationship situation that had been troubling me for sometime. In exasperation, she said: "Karen, just let go and let God handle this." I can still remember feeling both offended and hurt that she wasn't supporting my point of view. After all, she knew him. I wanted her to be angry along with me. Although it was a long time before I began to appreciate her suggestion fully, I now treasure it. In fact, as I have aged, it comforts me even more.

When I adhere to it, the idea of letting go immediately softens the moment of my discontent. The inner urge I feel to control a situation, a person, or the outcome of whatever has drawn my attention because of my fear still rears its ugly head, unfortunately. And sometimes I allow it to trigger a reaction. I'm sure this need to control developed very early in my life, no doubt because of my crippling insecurity. Fear is always the culprit, I think, when the drive to control takes root. And once it does, it monopolizes our thoughts.

When I look back on my life, I have to admit that I was born into a family of insecure, fear-filled controllers. My dad's anger was generally related to some situation or to one of us he was intent on controlling. When it came to controlling me, however, he failed. And I tried to keep him from controlling other family members as well, although unsuccessfully. My efforts, while sincere, were not helpful to anyone.

Fear can be a terrible burden to carry for a lifetime—a burden that can force us to feel a need for perfection and a need to control outcomes. In fact, I believe that the drive to control is synonymous with fear. But I also believe that, as long as we don't drop the hand of God, we are capable of experiencing fear's opposite: *peace*. Dropping the hand of God can happen so unconsciously for many of us. Even after more than forty years of walking a spiritual path, I sometimes too easily forget that God is my constant companion and that, more important, I have to choose to remember His Presence in order to call on His help. This really shouldn't be a hard thing to remember, but in my experience, it is. Sadly, it is.

I recall my mother-in-law telling me decades ago, when I was once again in the throes of debilitating fear and depression, that, if I felt far from God, it wasn't because God had moved. He never leaves your side, she softly reminded me. Soon after this conversation, she gave me a small refrigerator magnet that said: "If you feel far from God, He didn't move." That stayed on my refrigerator for many years. She also gave me a little blue book titled *The Practice of the Presence of God* by Brother Lawrence. I read and reread that book. I wanted his words to become imprinted on my mind. I longed for the constant awareness of God's presence while doing all my mundane daily chores, just as was true for him.

Ego Management

If you keep track, even for a day, of what happens when you remember to *just let go* and trust all outcomes to God, you will be far more eager to practice this suggestion whenever the ego tempts you into thinking "it's my turn now." The ego won't ever give up. That you can be sure of. It's very reason for existing is to take charge of your actions. But you don't have to let it take charge, and you have the tools to stop it.

We don't ever have to give up on the idea of letting go. And it feels so much more comforting and doable the more we practice it. In fact, we have multiple opportunities every day to let go of one thing or another—one person or another, one moment or another. Letting go never leads to a stressful situation. On the contrary, whatever situation has ensnared your ego will simply melt away. It really will. What can be better than that?

This book contains tried and true principles that have never failed to work for me as long as I remembered to utilize them. That's the hard part. *Remembering!* And the practice of just letting go may be the most potent of them all. It's simple, but seldom easy. It's easy to remember how to apply this principle, but hard to remember to use it. Yet in truth, it's always so easily accessible. Just three little words that can change any experience in the blink of an eye. Any experience.

Take an inventory of all the successes you've had when trying to apply this principle. You will remember a few

failures, no doubt; in fact, I still experience failures, sometimes daily. But focusing on your successes will make it far
easier to turn this principle into a steady habit. What we
focus on grows in strength. This is an absolute. Reflecting on our lives demonstrates this. Try keeping track of all
those experiences in which you allowed yourself to let go
for one week. Then note how surrendering made you feel.
By becoming aware of the benefits of letting go, you will
become far more willing to practice it. Over and over.

We have all acquired plenty of bad habits in our life-
times. In fact, it is probably true that all twenty of the principles in this book were born out of bad habits that I nurtured
over many years. Fortunately, our bad habits always have
the potential of being reversed. When we commit unwaver-
ingly to breaking the habit of controlling others, letting go
of them instead so that God can take charge, we can change
our behavior and change our lives.

And this behavior will set an example for others, showing them that letting go is not only possible but doable, if
only we work at it. What a worthy outcome we can achieve
from just a bit of practice. And what a gift to all the individuals we walk among.

I have no idea where any of you are on your journeys
through life. I don't know if you are 12-Steppers, or on
another spiritual path, or on no spiritual path at all. Maybe
you were simply drawn to this book because of the title, or
because you have read another of my books.

I don't know if you are young and searching for a simpler
life or drawing to the close of life as I am. At eighty, I am
certainly well into the last quarter of my life. I'm assuming
that's why writing this particular book was so appealing to
me. I love reflecting on what I have learned throughout my

journey. This process affirms that there have been no accidents, no superfluous experiences or lessons along the way. Every single experience flowed quite perfectly, if not always smoothly, into the next one. This will remain true until my journey is complete. And it will be true for you as well, I think.

I have no idea at the moment if this book will be my last. I doubt it, actually. But I do know that opting for a simpler, more peaceful life has called to me. And I'm thinking it has called to you as well, or you would not have been drawn to this book.

Reviewing any number of the simple principles that I have embraced over the years for finding a softer, more serene and loving life led me to select the particular principles you find in this book as the things I know for sure. There were many I could have chosen, of course. But these stood out in my mind for the ease with which they can actually be practiced.

In all honesty, they chose me. I think that's not uncommon as we wend our way through life. The experiences we need to have find us. The people we need to meet come calling. The lessons we have agreed to incorporate into our lives will come, and come again if necessary, until we surrender to them. Learning to let go is just another one of those lessons—perhaps the most valuable one of all.

Surrendering to what is makes that which lies before us so much more acceptable, tolerable, and manageable. As I see it, surrendering goes hand-in-hand with letting go. And that doesn't mean sullenly giving up. On the contrary. Surrendering means that we say, "Okay. I understand. You are in charge and all is well." To me, surrendering feels like taking a deep breath and being recharged. It elicits an inner joy.

And we certainly all deserve as much inner joy as we can cultivate. To think that joy is as accessible as breathing is an awesome prospect, as I see it.

If letting go doesn't lift your spirits, then go ahead and hang on. But I think that, in time, you will grow weary of attempting to control that which will never be controlled. Your opportunity is to let go and live free from the tension that your attempts to control others creates in your body. Please note that I said *attempts* to control others. Our actions in this regard are never more than attempts. We simply don't have the capacity to make anyone else conform to our will. Not even children, actually. And certainly, when it comes to the relationship partners in our lives—those who are significant as well as those who are fleeting—trying to control someone's behavior, opinions, or experience is not in either our best interests or theirs. It's a burden that comes with no reward.

The journey each of us is here to make is shaped by a Higher Power. And neither you nor I can be someone else's Higher Power. How lucky we are that the burden of others' lives is not our responsibility. How lucky we are that "just letting go" is an option that can provide a clear path to peace of mind. How lucky we are that our paths can be far simpler and more peaceful than we may have thought earlier in our lives.

May you all find the peace for which you yearn. May you all celebrate the power of letting go of all those individuals you walk among. They will appreciate you for it. And you will realize that it is the very lesson you were drawn together to experience. Perhaps the one and only lesson.

20 Things I Know for Sure

CLOSING THOUGHTS

Coming to the close of a book I have loved writing is always bittersweet for me. I'm gently relieved that closure called to me, but I'm also sad to say goodbye to my process of sharing these specific ideas that have so clearly been the guiding posts in my own life. I cultivated and then have lived with these particular principles for many, many years and they have never betrayed me. I'm quite confident they never will. And this idea thrills me. To have a set of beliefs I can always count on to undergird my journey through any situation is the gift of contentment.

It's my deepest hope that you found a few principles among these twenty that you can embrace as well. I think we all deserve softer, far more gentle lives. We all deserve a bit of simplicity to walk us through each day. We all deserve to know that life doesn't need to trouble us constantly. We all need to become aware of the importance of each experience as the next necessary opportunity for our growth.

If you remember only one thing from this book, I hope it's that your journey has been both intentional and truly divine. You have never been forgotten or led astray. God is now and always was present. We don't have to feel His Presence for this to be true.

As I said many times throughout the book, I didn't suddenly become peaceful. And I'm not always peaceful now. Far from it. But through daily practice of these principles, my life has become what I had always hoped it would be—on most days. I appreciate the upward trajectory of my path and can see that I'm headed where I need to be moment by moment. What a glorious realization that is. What helps me daily is adherence, as much as possible, to the following beliefs:

- There are two voices in my mind: one is always wrong, always trying to create chaos where none need be; the other is quietly loving and will always lead me on a softer journey, which also means that everyone I encounter will be treated more gently as well.

- Wherever I am, I am meant to be. I believe the same is true for you.

- All healing happens within our relationships, the good ones and the more troubled ones. And not overnight either! In fact, our more difficult relationships may be far more advantageous to our spiritual growth.

- Our lessons are specific and we readily agreed to them before our birth into this life. While we can put off learning any lesson for as long as we want, it will patiently wait for us to be ready.

- Every person on my path is a teacher. For this, I am very grateful. And relieved.

- Nothing is more fruitful than forgiveness. We can have no inner peace without it.

- There is no struggle so big or so important that it cannot be relinquished.

- My journey is always with God. And this is true for you as well.

- Being helpful to others, any others, is our primary purpose in this life.

- Changing our perspective is the surest way to change our lives. All you have to say is, "Help me see this differently," and calm will settle over you.

- Simply not being derailed by the ego's incessant call is pure pleasure—and a constant choice.

- Choosing to see peace rather than the chaos that is often so glaring changes everything.

- It's never helpful to see ourselves as separate from others. That's what initiates judgment.

- Seeking to see a troubling situation differently changes us completely.

- Every loving thought is true. Every other expression from anyone is a call for healing and help.

- We must cherish the gift of "just letting go." It eases our minds instantly and reduces any tension we feel.

- Giving all outcomes over to God comforts us completely. Our job is simply to be kind.

- Any experience we have with anyone is what that person has chosen to experience as well. We made a sacred contract to experience the lesson together before being born.

And I believe that all will be well. All will *always* be well.

I would love to hear from you regarding how your life has changed as the result of applying some of the principles in this book. I honestly do believe that you can become willing to shift how you think and behave with a bit of practice. It's my hope—my prayer, actually—that you will enjoy greater peace in all your tomorrows. The peace any one of us feels gets expressed in very subtle ways, and the universe always takes notice. *Always*.

Peace be with you, now.
Karen

Please write to me at karencasey@me.com

ACKNOWLEDGMENTS

There are many people, from both my present and my past, who deserve a huge nod of thanks. My husband, Joe, comes first to mind. We have been traveling this road together for more than forty years and I can always rely on him for honesty, guidance, kindness, and loving support.

All my friends in AA and Al-Anon also come quickly to mind. Without their constant presence, my life would have upended decades ago.

I'm also indebted to the millions of readers of my books, and the thousands of them who have contacted me through snail mail, email, phone calls, texts, and workshops since my first book "hit the stands" in 1982. You will never know how much your messages have meant to me.

I certainly can't forget Jan Johnson, who brought me to Red Wheel/Weiser as an author for the publication of *Change Your Mind and Your Life Will Follow*. She was kind and so supportive of my work. My journey with Red Wheel has been a marvelous "marriage" ever since.

And thanks to Greg Brandenburgh and Christine LeBlond, who have helped me through the editing channels of late. And Jane Hagaman, you held my hand when I most needed it. All authors owe their editors a debt of gratitude for making their work better in every way.

And I would be remiss if I didn't thank all my friends at Hazelden who saw my potential as a writer many decades ago. Linda Peterson was the first to be instrumental in taking me by the hand. Becky Post and Pat Benson, too, kept me on track and uplifted. And numerous others walked by my side for years. You know who you are. I love you one and all.

20 Things I Know for Sure

ABOUT THE AUTHOR

Karen Casey is a writer and workshop facilitator for 12-step recovery. Her first book, *Each Day a New Beginning*, has sold more than 3 million copies. She has published 28 books since then, including *Change Your Mind and Your Life Will Follow*, which was a finalist for Books for a Better Life Award. Visit her at *www.womens-spirituality.com*.

TO OUR READERS

Conari Press, an imprint of Red Wheel/Weiser, publishes books on topics ranging from spirituality, personal growth, and relationships to women's issues, parenting, and social issues. Our mission is to publish quality books that will make a difference in people's lives—how we feel about ourselves and how we relate to one another. We value integrity, compassion, and receptivity, both in the books we publish and in the way we do business.

Our readers are our most important resource, and we appreciate your input, suggestions, and ideas about what you would like to see published.

Visit our website at *www.redwheelweiser.com* to learn about our upcoming books and free downloads, and be sure to go to *www.redwheelweiser.com/newsletter* to sign up for newsletters and exclusive offers.

You can also contact us at *info@rwwbooks.com*.

Conari Press
an imprint of Red Wheel/Weiser, LLC
65 Parker Street, Suite 7
Newburyport, MA 01950
www.redwheelweiser.com